Language Experiences For All Students

Nancy Hansen-Krening

Addison-Wesley Publishing Company

Menlo Park, California · Reading, Massachusetts
London · Amsterdam · Don Mills, Ontario · Sydney

For Elisabeth Whittier Hansen—
mother, friend, and mentor—
the wisest person I know.
For Miranda Harrison Whittier, grandmother;
and Nancy Margaret Harrison, great-grandmother—
each woman fought the battle in her own way,
and in her own way,
made the path easier for me to follow.

This book is published by the Addison-Wesley Innovative Division.

The photograph on page 228 (and on the back cover) is by Tom McMackin.

All other photographs are by Jonathan Clark.

Illustrations and design by Barbara Clark.

Copyright © 1982 by Addison-Wesley Publishing Company, Inc. All rights reserved. Printed in the United States of America. Published simultaneously in Canada.

ISBN 0-201-03912-5
ABCDEFGHIJKL-ML-8765432

Preface

Fourteen years ago, I moved into a new school district and a new grade level. After teaching junior high school language arts and reading, and later, teaching fourth grade, I was returning to first grade.

I was welcomed to the school and first grade by my new principal, Gordon L. Corner. It was Mr. Corner who introduced me to Evawynne Spriggs. Both people changed my life forever—and certainly for the better!

Evawynne taught first grade next door to my own classroom (at that time, she became my son's first grade teacher). She, with Mr. Corner's unflagging support, gave me the courage and knowledge to teach Language Experience. It was on-the-job training.

The word *courage* describes what I felt I needed. There was no teacher's manual to put words in my mouth, no reading groups in which to neatly niche my students. There was just me, my knowledge of the children, and their knowledge of language and experience. How challenging, exciting, and terrifying! But it worked, and I have never turned back nor lost my faith in Language Experience.

Over the past seven years since leaving the public school classroom for the university classroom, I have met and worked with many bright, creative, competent teachers. They have been interested in teaching Language Experience, but they have also asked for guidelines. They wanted an organized, skills-based structure that would help them start a Language Experience reading and language arts program. I have understood this concern. I would have felt more secure in teaching Language Experience had I begun with concrete guidelines.

As I have given inservice workshops and demonstration teaching with children for classroom teachers, ESL teachers and special education teachers, as I have taught summer workshops, and as I have worked as a consultant on Language Experience and Language Development, I have gradually developed such a basic skills structure. This book represents both that skills-based guideline and my years of practical experience as a teacher. It is my hope that teachers of *all* children will find it helpful. However much or little you use from this book, please remember that Language Experience stimulates the growth of power in our students. Power in communication, thinking, problem solving, as well as the power that results from respecting and valuing others, is the power of survival.

There are many fine people who have contributed to this book. The children who shared their intelligence, creativity, sensitivity, and trust will live forever in my memory. Fellow teachers and faithful friends, Peggy Gittins and Louise Carlson, shared with me the daily excitement (and occasional frustration) of teaching. These two dear friends continue to share their classes with me. Ellen Kletzock, our school secretary, often paved the way for me and for the children. Diane Collum, Katy Spangler, and Jane Brem, trusted sisters, shared the laughter and tears of my life as I wrote. Katy provided skilled editing. Sandra Emilia Gonzales, my surrogate daughter and adviser, helped me with so many details. Pat Bonner typed and organized material with friendship, patience, and expertise. Peggy Maroney protected my time for writing.

My very special son is Eric Timothy, whose beautiful guitar music, perceptive listening, and sensitive comments stimulated and encouraged me as I wrote. His Language Experience stories appear in this book as well as in my last book. Sylvia Ashton-Warner's books and life are a constant inspiration. James A. Banks, scholar and friend, always expresses interest in my work. Dean James Doi's appreciation of scholarly work is gratefully acknowledged. C.A. Bowers is a brilliant person who has effected permanent change in my thinking. And Dianne Monson, a colleague of intelligence who models excellence in all she does. I owe special appreciation to my mother, Elisabeth Whittier Hansen, for her painstaking corrections of the copy-edited manuscipt. And finally, mizpah to both my parents, Elisabeth and Jan, who love and support me, no matter what I do!

Contents

5   Independent Reading and Writing: Step A   99

6   Independent Reading and Writing: Step B   131

9

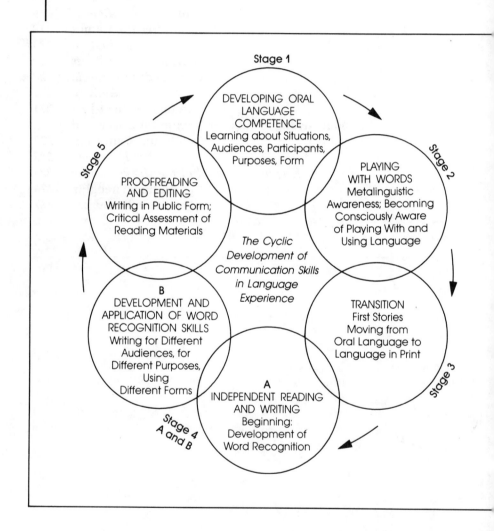

Stage 1

DEVELOPING ORAL
LANGUAGE
COMPETENCE
Learning about Situations,
Audiences, Participants,
Purposes, Form

Stage 5

PROOFREADING
AND EDITING
Writing in Public Form;
Critical Assessment of
Reading Materials

Stage 2

PLAYING
WITH WORDS
Metalinguistic
Awareness; Becoming
Consciously Aware
of Playing With and
Using Language

The Cyclic
Development of
Communication Skills
in Language
Experience

B
DEVELOPMENT AND
APPLICATION OF WORD
RECOGNITION SKILLS
Writing for Different
Audiences, for
Different Purposes,
Using
Different Forms

TRANSITION
First Stories
Moving from
Oral Language to
Language in Print

Stage 3

A
INDEPENDENT READING
AND WRITING
Beginning:
Development of
Word Recognition

Stage 4
A and B

The cyclic development of communication skills in language experience

Introduction

Within each communication act, we respond as individuals. Our personal, unique stamp emerges in even the most formal, impersonal situations. *That* is our strength. Uniqueness asserts our identity. It is in this sense that Language Experience is for all students. By drawing upon, developing, and preserving the individual world views of each student, self-identity remains intact. As an approach to developing thinking skills, and reading and language arts skills, Language Experience consistently focuses upon expanding the natural abilities of each child according to the child's singular competencies.

In this approach each student—second language learners as well as mainstreamed learners included—succeeds. No one fails. Using a child's own language, a child's own response to shared experiences precludes finding a child deficient in language, knowledge, or experience. Each performs according to individual capabilities. Since the child reads what the child has written (or dictated for the teacher to write), the words are known and flow naturally. I believe that it is crucial that we, as teachers, nurture and build upon the strengths of our students. That should seem infinitely reasonable to all of us, since we grow best when we receive recognition for what we *can* do. As teachers, we often say to ourselves, "I wish they would talk about what we can do rather than always complaining about what they think we can't or don't do." The constant criticisms by the media, parents and legislators drain us of enthusiasm and sometimes even dull our desire to achieve. Well, the same thing occurs with students.

The Language Experience Approach

The Language Experience Approach uses each child's own language and response to experiences in developing the competent performance of basic skills in listening, speaking, reading, writing, and problem solving. Language Experience Approach (LEA) uses each child's own language to record the child's responses to personal, primary group, school experiences. There is a sequence to any Language Experience lesson:

First: Teacher plans a shared experience for the class.

Second: Students become directly involved in the experience.

Third: A student responds orally to experience.

Fourth: A student responds by writing (or the teacher writes what student dictates).

Fifth: A student reads the written response.

As you can see, the Language Experience Approach is a holistic approach to teaching basic language arts and reading skills. Initially, the teacher elicits the student's language through individual and group discussions of experiences. These experiences are both out-of-school experiences as well as experiences planned by the teacher. As Language Experience progresses, the teacher records the student's ideas, thoughts, creations in print. The dictated stories and, later, student-written stories provide reading materials.

It is inherent that in this approach all students are overtly valued for the language experiences they bring to the classroom. This is not a static valuing because the teacher is also responsible for introducing new experiences and new language skills. Through individual and class discussions, teachers, students, and peers provide labels for new and old concepts. Students are, by the very nature of this approach, required to think about the work with familiar and unfamiliar concepts, the language attached to those concepts, and the skills needed to generalize both concepts and skills.

As you can see from the preceding diagram, learning is a cyclical, interactive process. As language skills and concepts grow, students are capable of understanding more of what they hear, see, and read. The process constantly expands; it is never static. The arrows indicate that learning is not linear; all of the stages interact with each other. As the student grows within a stage, the power of the student as a communicator also grows. The child who reaches Stage 5 is more powerful than a Stage 1 child. *But*, a Stage 5 student who repeats the cycle is even more powerful than either. Although a child may enter at any point in the cycle, continued experiences with Stages 1, 2, 4, and 5 should be planned.

Language Experience for Second Language Learners

Language Experience provides a practical, common sense approach to teaching English as a second language.

Since research has discovered the intimate relationship between first and second language learning, we realize the importance of providing a language-rich, experience-based learning environment for the acquisition of a new language. Language Experience insures that the child can develop and grow in a positive, supportive atmosphere, which provides opportunities to learn a new language within the context of need and use.

The first stage of language learning is, naturally, a quiet time for most people. It is a time of listening, watching, and absorbing a new language within its experiential context. The language learner uses this time to develop a receptive repertoire of language—one which greatly exceeds the learner's expressive production. Often, the child will understand and process sentences and strings of sentences, but in talking will use only one or two words to express a complete thought. Language Experience provides the opportunity for each learner to hear and see language used in a variety of ways for a variety of purposes *in context*. The valuing of one, two, and three word utterances, according them as much respect as more complex utterances, encourages the child to continue to use language. Children feel safe to experiment with and produce new words. Consistent trying out of the second language stimulates growth toward the second stage of language learning.

The second stage of language learning is one of practicing and using words and sentences. The learner can label and classify experiences with simple sentences, usually in the present tense. Code switching between first and second languages is not unusual. Again, the participants in the communication act must respond to the content of expression rather than the form or fluency of speech. At this point, Language Experience stories progress from the dictation of one, two, or three word labels to entire sentences. By encouraging the practice and use of language, the teacher provides opportunities for second language learners to progress to the third stage of language learning.

Stage three is the purposeful use of language in conversation, discussion and creative expression. The student possesses a large enough vocabulary in the second language to actively participate in story writing and reading. At this point, the student begins spontaneously to correct that form in communication—and may even extend that correction to other second language learners! Code switching still happens, but usually from deliberate choice rather than from lack of knowledge.

By encouraging these abilities, these strengths in discussion, creative dramatics and story writing, the teacher stimulates the child's progression to the fourth stage of language acquisition. At this stage, children use language for hypothesizing, and manipulating ideas—a most abstract skill since it relies on words and thoughts rather than specific, concrete activities. Within the developmental sequence of Language Experience, Stage 1 second language learners would be involved in Stages 1 and 2 in the Language Experience cycle. Stage 2 learners would fall in Stage 3 Language Experience. Stage 3 and 4 learners would be Stage 4 and 5 Language Experience learners.

The following is a level-by-level reading and language arts guideline I developed for a workshop in Texas. I have used the four stages of oral language competency as organizers. These are suggested guidelines for planning instruction for second language learners. Please remember that the stages are flexible. Children can demonstrate skills from a variety of stages. Your key for instruction is to plan lessons at the child's competency stage. That is, use the stage where the child's characteristic behaviors form a cluster.

LANGUAGE ARTS

Stage 1

Listens to others talk
Uses 1, 2 and 3 words to communicate entire concepts
Responds well to peer teaching and buddies' directions
Can combine pictures and other visual stimuli with 1, 2 and 3 word labels
Needs many opportunities to hear spoken language, using a variety of forms for different purposes
Needs survival language
Can learn from songs and chants
Can pantomime
Enjoys art and can provide 1–3 word labels for artistic creations
Enjoys working with rhythms

Stage 2

Listens carefully and begins to speak more and more, especially in small groups
Can work with rhymes *and* rhythms
Needs continued teacher direction

Continues to rely on buddies
Can dictate 3–5 word sentences that tell and describe rather than explain
Can put together simple stories
Can write brief invitations
Code switches
Can help write simple reports
Can give brief oral reports that tell a sequence of events
Enjoys role playing and acting out stories
Uses present tense almost exclusively

Stage 3
Listen and speaks purposively
Uses language for concrete problem solving in discussion, reporting and questioning
Can give oral and written reports based on conceptualization of old and new information
Can use both present and past tenses when needed
Can begin to write independently with less teacher direction
Spontaneous expression of self with greater confidence
Can debate looking at both sides of an issue
Can distinguish between functional and creative writing
Can perform operations with syntax (substitutions, deletions, rearrangements)
Can write poetry
Can dramatize
Understands the need to use language that is appropriate for audience and situation

Stage 4
Develops power in communication by anticipating audience
Selects language (verbal and written) that is most effective for a given audience
Can label and manipulate parts of speech
Proofreads and edits
Uses a variety of forms for a variety of purposes (essays, poems, debates, plays, short stories)
Can analyze the writings of others

READING

Stage 1
Needs to hear stories—every day—in English
Needs to see the association between spoken word and printed word
Enjoys "reading" wordless picture books and colorful magazines
Listens to taped stories
Can read 1 and 2 word labels
Can read own name
Can label simple science experiments
Can point to locations on maps and globes
Can play simple word and alphabet games
Enjoys learning songs and chants

Stage 2

Is ready for the Language Experience Approach to Reading
Can develop sight word vocabulary
Can begin to read simple 3–5 word sentences written in present tense (not limited to LEA stories, includes basal readers and trade books)
Older students can begin to dictate LEA stories for science and social studies
Can work with simple context clues
Can sequence events
Can retell stories at recall level

Stage 3

Can learn high utility phonics generalizations
Can read from basal series or trade books
Can use inferential reading skills and answer comprehension questions at the inferential level
Gradually progresses to independent reading
Can move into reading in the content areas, but may need advance, conceptual organizers

Stage 4

A critical reader
Can identify biased, prejudicial language
Can predict alternative outcomes
Can hypothesize beyond the ending of the story
Needs to analyze different forms and purposes of writing
An independent reader

Language Experience for Children with Special Needs

Mainstreamed students must feel that they are accepted, valued, sharing members of the class. When students use and share their language and experience as the basis for developing communication skills, the approach itself tells all the students that they are important. Language Experience focuses on individual worth in a shared group context. It brings all students together through sharing, through communicating.

Because of the flexible nature of a Language Experience classroom, modifying the physical organization of desks, tables, chalkboards and work areas is part of the routine. Consequently, a child with a physical disability can be accommodated in the natural order of things. Rooms can be arranged to provide for wheelchairs, to allow for optimum positioning for hearing and seeing. This is accomplished with no fuss and bother. Disabled children need never feel that they are singled out as a source of disruption.

In a Language Experience classroom, visually impaired students have many opportunities to manipulate concrete objects. This increases both receptive and expressive language growth. Using media such as clay for illustrations stimulates the creative abilities of children with limited vision.

Dictating stories to the teacher, an aide, peers or any helper in the room is a natural component of Language Experience. Children with impaired vision as well as children who have difficulty holding pencils can dictate their stories without feeling singled out for being different. The stories can be typed or printed with large letters, or they can be printed in Braille as part of the daily writing process.

Hearing impaired children can dictate either through talking or by using sign language. If they use oral language in telling their stories, the focus will be on listening to what they are saying, not upon their ability to articulate specific sounds.

Mainstreaming often involves educating the rest of the class in order for them to understand and respect the rights and the abilities of either learning disabled or physically disabled children. Language Experience draws upon the thoughts and experiences of student authors; the entire class then learns to appreciate the realities of their disabled peers. There are frequent informal and formal occasions through which life experiences can be shared and discussed in a respectful environment.

The chapter on oral language focuses specifically on hearing impaired students. This population of youngsters seems to represent a great concern for teachers. We all want to facilitate communication between all students and adults, but we must first have knowledge about a disability that may require special attention from the teacher. Teaching oral communication skills to a hearing impaired child does require special knowledge on the part of the classroom teacher.

The other chapters are more general in discussing children with special needs. It would be impossible to identify every special need that may require extra planning. For example, my son is plagued with severe allergies. When these allergies are active, his learning and performance are significantly reduced. Also, my mother has had severe arthritis since she was sixteen. When her joints are inflamed, the extreme pain influences everything she does. Because of these personal experiences and a deep interest, I would be inclined to single-out allergies and arthritis as disabilities that need special planning. But that would leave many equally important disabilities untouched. Consequently, I have attempted to present ideas that can be adopted and/or adapted for all children with special needs.

The lessons for children who need extra consideration are not intended to isolate them from whole class instruction; they are to be used *in addition* to the other lessons. A child who is physically mainstreamed deserves to be included with whole-class instruction.

Multicultural Experiences and Desegregation

Classrooms across the nation reflect the diversity of ethnic group memberships. Desegregation and equal opportunity in employment have been contributing factors in integrating children in classrooms. But whether or not a classroom reflects ethnic diversity, materials used for learning must do so. We live in a world that will survive only if we learn about and try our best to understand the lives and values of people from whom we differ. This means that we must all learn from and about each other. Gaining knowledge about others, one's peers, is natural when we communicate using our language to express our views of shared and individual experiences. This is a beginning in creating mutual understanding. Students who write stories about their families, and about out-of-school experiences, bring their lives into the classroom. Students who write stories, poetry, and songs about their view of the world add to the knowledge and understanding of others. Teachers who bring resource people into the classroom, who use films, pictures, books, tapes and records that reflect many cultures, expand the cultural and ethnic literacy of themselves and their students. Language Experience necessitates talking, sharing, and listening by students and teacher alike. It opens communication channels. It helps us learn about each other.

Organization of the Book

The chapters in this book are organized to represent the step-by-step progression of the Language Experience Approach for both primary and intermediate grades. For example, Chapter 2, *Developing Oral Language Competence*, identifies basic oral language skills and then presents lessons which may be used to develop those skills. Each chapter also includes specific sets of lessons for second language learners as well as sets of lessons for mainstreamed students. For the latter student population, teachers should work first with those specific lesson plans *and then select additional lessons from the first part of the chapter*. These lessons provide additional steps in the developmental progression, consequently, since special lessons are placed at the end of the chapters. Teachers of special populations would reverse the order using those lessons first and then use the lessons planned for the total classroom as mainstreaming lessons. I have classified the bulk of the lessons and all of the basic skills as being either for "Beginning Learners" or "Intermediate Learners." Generally, this indicates a distinction between primary grades (K-3) and intermediate grades (4–6). I avoided specific grade designation because it could be misleading since most of the lessons can be used for people of varying ages. Certainly students beyond the age of twelve could learn communication skills from these lessons. In fact, an instructor in occupational therapy has used some of the lessons in helping people learn how to talk. So you can consider the designations as probable skill levels rather than age or grade levels.

Chapter 3, *Playing with Words: Metalinguistic Awareness,* presents lessons for developing the students' ability to look at spoken and printed language as a symbol system that they can *consciously* manipulate. This awareness precedes the conceptualization of word recognition skills and critical listening, reading and writing skills.

Chapter 4, *Transition: First Stories,* explains how to make the transition from oral language to language in print. Few intermediate grade teachers would need to read this chapter in depth, although most would need to consider the lessons for special populations.

Chapters 5 and 6, *Independent Reading and Writing: Steps A and B,* are companion chapters. They describe the process teachers and students plan and implement in progressing from varying degrees of dependency on others for dictation and spelling to total self-reliance in writing. These chapters also present the transition from reading and Language Experience stories to reading commercially printed books.

Chapter 7, *Proofreading and Editing,* outlines lessons that emphasize the use of standard spelling, mechanics, usage, and writing conventions. At this point, the importance of form receives major stress. All children must learn public forms of communication in order to gain credibility with reading audiences.

You will note that most chapters start with a listing of basic skills that will be taught through the Language Experience lessons. Listings for intermediate grades and primary grades are printed on separate pages. This does not mean, however, that either set of teachers should not read all of the listings. We certainly know by now that children vary so greatly in individual abilities that grade lines are artificial. Primary grade teachers will need to increase their expectations for skill building with gifted students—just as intermediate grade teachers must plan to meet the needs of students who have missed out on learning necessary skills, skills that are usually learned at an earlier grade level.

Chapter 8, *Organizing,* is a pivotal chapter. For some of you, it might be best to begin with this chapter. Often teachers feel that Language Experience presents serious organizational obstacles. This is not so. If teachers plan carefully, if they structure their planning efficiently, teaching Language Experience is a breeze. I have seen first year teachers do a terrific job with Language Experience. In fact, Ellen, one of the most outstanding first year teachers I have known, said to me, "Don't you dare tell people that Language Experience presents too many organizational problems for new teachers!" I won't.

Chapter 9, *Finally* . . ., includes some closing remarks.

Language Experience and Language Growth

All students have individual abilities, backgrounds, levels of language development and approaches to learning. In addition to meeting the realities of these needs, teachers of reading and language arts face unprecedented demands upon their knowledge and teaching strategies. In addition to working with traditional populations of students, teachers must now expand their planning to include teaching children with a variety of special needs.

While working with an increasingly diverse classroom, teachers are also facing the demands of teaching a standardized set of basic skills. By broadening our understanding of language learning, we can cope with those demands. If we consider the requirements of a language learning environment, we see the importance of using a program such as Language Experience. Judith Lindfors states, ". . . some aspects of language and its acquisition are, I believe, so deeply rooted and pervasive that they cut across the specifics of setting, age and role, and thus have implications for us." (Lindfors, Judith. *Children's Language and Learning*. Englewood Cliffs: Prentice-Hall, 1980.) If you think about the aspects of language learning that Lindfors identifies, you will quickly understand the need to implement Language Experience in your classroom. A summary of those aspects includes:

1. The growth of language is a continuous process for children.
2. The growth of language is deeply rooted in the child's cognitive growth.
3. The growth of language involves the child as an active party in the learning process.
4. The growth of language is aided by an environment which is geared toward the child's way of learning.
5. The growth of language is aided by an environment which is responsive to the child.
6. The growth of language is aided by an environment which focuses on meaning rather than form.
7. The growth of language is aided by an environment which provides rich diversity of verbal and nonverbal experience. (ibid.)

Assessing Readiness for Language Experience

Tell me about your picture, Anna.
Dog.
Can you tell me some more about your dog?
Big.
How big is your dog?
Big.

or

Tell me about your picture, Louisa.
This is me and my momma.
What are you and your momma doing?
Kissing.
Okay, what do you want me to write about you
and your momma?
This is me and my momma.

Contrary to many teachers' concerns, all children do not talk on and on in either conversation or story dictation language experience stories. Some will respond with one or two word labels (Anna) while others give simple, five-six word statements (Louisa). Neither child is deficient. Statements such as these should be accepted as a possible indicator of the child's present stage of oral language production. We must listen to oral language and plan lessons that will stimulate its growth. In LEA, we plan verbal interaction within the context of actual experience. All of the lessons in this book are based on the premise that children will develop an expanding, powerful knowledge that our ability to use language in different situations with different participants, for different purposes using different forms creates self-sufficient communicators.

Teachers of young children must assume initial responsibility in assessing the child's existing level of oral language production. Without a basic knowledge of the child's base-line ability, we may create frustration; furthermore, we have no concrete knowledge for planning further language growth. Otherwise, we have what Cazden terms "broadcast" teaching.

Teaching may be conceived as one kind of communication for which role taking—in the sense of assessing the abilities, needs, and motivations of another—is essential. Adapting one's message to individual children admittedly requires more effort than an unrecoded broadcast to a group, and looking for and using the feedback provided by the reactions of one's listener(s) is hard work too. (Cazden, Courtney. *Child Language and Education.* New York: Holt, Rinehart and Winston, 1972.)

Practical experience led me to develop the following informal method of assessing individual, oral language production. If it will help you, feel free to use it in your classes.

Assessing Oral Language Production

First, Concrete Description

Language Experience draws upon the ability of students to describe their own experiences. In a developmental progression, children rely

| | Child's Name: _____ |
| | Age: _____ |

ASSESSING ORAL LANGUAGE PRODUCTION

CONCRETE DESCRIPTION	Label	Descriptive Units	ABSTRACT DESCRIPTION	Specific Example	Functional Use	Concept	CREATIVE DESCRIPTION
			book				
			picture				
			story				
			print				
			word				
			line				
			think				
			letter				
			name				
			write				
			learn				Comments
Comments			draw				
			page				
			read				
			number				
			Comments				

upon the actual presence of the concrete object in order to describe that object. If you expect a child to describe a pictorial representation of people, places, and things, you must first assess the child's ability to describe *concrete* objects.

Second, Abstract Description

As teachers we necessarily use nouns—such as *book, picture, story*—as well as verbs—such as *draw, print, read*. Through my own teaching as well as through observations and teacher surveys in other classrooms, I determined a list of high frequency words teachers use in working with Language Experience. The list is used to establish the individual child's meaning of words used in instruction. These are words for which we *assume* similar meanings for child and teacher. In both pilot testing and field testing Assessing Oral Language Production,[1] I discovered that the bulk of child meanings are based upon the function of that word. The next most frequent level of defining was through the use of specific example (direct referent). The third most frequent response was, "I don't know." (One child said, "My mouth doesn't have that word yet.") Very few children verbalized a conceptualization (generalization) of the listed words. In practical terms, this means that you should start the year by assessing student meaning for instructional terms. To do otherwise can put roadblocks in student learning. I know; I did this more than once. Early on in teaching first grade, I had just introduced the idea of conferencing the children, and I set times for individual conferences. That night, as they gathered for their goodbye hugs, I gave Larry an extra squeeze and said, "Oh, boy! Tomorrow you get to read." Larry was a terrific little boy, brimming with enthusiasm and love, an energetic delight. Early the next morning I received a frantic call from Larry's mother. Larry was in tears. He stoutly refused to go to school. I was totally stunned. Larry finally agreed to come to the phone. Between sniffs and gulps, he said, "I can't read. I can't know all of those words in books." Well, what had happened was that Larry defined reading as knowing *all* of the words in every book. He did not associate reading with decoding his own Language Experience books. I could tell you innumerable stories that vividly and sometimes painfully illustrate the differences between what you mean and what children understand.

Third, Creative Description

Language Experience is based on the child's ability to spontaneously generate a creative description of an actual or imagined experience.

---

[1] At that time, I called it Language Acquisition Coding Descriptor.

Before beginning Language Experience, you need to know how experienced children are at creating stories. You also need to know whether or not they use complete sentences in oral production.

Then, Putting It Together

The combined information of the first three categories will tell you the child's *existing* oral language base. This information will help you select and plan oral language lessons for your students. For example, if the student uses very little descriptive language, you should plan informal conversations where the child and a more verbally proficient peer are talking about and describing concrete objects as well as concrete experiences. Using and hearing language in a purposeful context develops language skills.

Information from the assessment also tells you what you may reasonably expect from the child. If information from the second category tells you that a student is tied to a specific example for word meaning, then you know that you must plan lessons that will expand the child's knowledge of the concept. A teacher learned that one of her little girls thought that a line was "something you get in to go some place."

"Can a line be on a paper?"

"Yes, if us kids stand on it."

For the first time the teacher understood why Martha gave her a skeptical look when she said, "Martha, your printing is messy. You must stay inside the lines." An absolutely true story!

Language Experience can foster cognitive development by consciously planning experiences (as this book does) that stimulate cognitive growth. But before any of this begins, you need to know the child's existing stage of development.

If a student cannot make up any sort of coherent story for the third category, then you know that person needs to *hear* stories. Also, that student needs lots of play with puppets, flannel-board characters, and dolls or stuffed animals. Participating in the pretend of dress-up, pantomime, creative movement and creative dramatics also stimulates creative expression.

Language Experience is based on student language; you must know where that language begins in order to facilitate growth.

Test Directions

The testing environment as well as the rapport or feeling between the student and the tester has a great deal to do with how much talking a student will produce. Because of this, I always precede individual assessment with whole-group activities. During this time, you can also observe whether or not there are children whose oral language production demonstrates no need for assessment. You will need to fill out a record sheet for each child before you begin the whole-group activities:

Category I: Concrete Description

Materials: Student record sheet and collections of small colorful objects such as blocks, plastic toys, pipe cleaners, rocks, pieces of cloth, wallpaper cut in different shapes.

Directions: Organize the class in sets of two or three. Give them time to look at and play with the materials. After a few minutes you can say, "We are going to play a game." Have children sit back to back so that neither partner can see each other's hands or lap. Divide the objects between partners.

Assign one child as the talker and one as the guesser. "We are going to play a guessing game. The talker is going to tell you everything about the object. The guesser must guess the name of the object." After the talker and guesser have played the game, reverse roles.

Allow enough time so that you can move from set to set listening to each child talk. To avoid restlessness, you may extend this game over two or three days. As you move through the room, you can note the children who obviously need no further assessment in this category. Note your decision on that child's record sheet.

For individual assessment, you will collect the objects you plan to use and list them in the blank spaces under Category I. When you work with the child, sit back to back so that the child knows that you *cannot* see what is being described. If the child knows that you *can* see the object, he may just point and say, "It has one of those things and this thing. . ."

If the child simply labels the object, note this *and then say,* "Remember, I can't see _____ . Does it have colors? Does it have parts?" In other words, encourage more language. (Note this under Comments). Put a checkmark for each descriptive word the child uses for the object.

Category II: Abstract Description

Materials: Student record sheet

Directions: Again, this should be introduced as a game, an *informal* situation (sitting on the floor with the children, sitting together at a table, or sitting in a circle). You can tell the children something such as, "You are going to play an outer-space game. You are very smart. But because you are from outer-space, you don't know the words teachers use in school. You need their help. You need to learn what words mean." Play the game by asking for the meaning of words such as *lunchroom, swing, school, principal, teacher.* Encourage the children to tell you more than a specific example.

You: *What is, 'teacher'?*

Class: *Mrs. Gittens.* (specific example)

You: *Oh, can only Mrs. Gittens be a teacher?*

Class: *No, people who teach school are teachers.* (functional use)

You: *Do you have to teach in a school to be a teacher?*

A student: *No, anyone who helps you learn something is a teacher.* (concept)

You: *Can a mother be a teacher?*

Class: *No, mothers take care of children.* (functional use)

A student: *Yes, if she helps you learn.* (concept)

During the class game time, you will note children who are operating consistently at a conceptual level, a functional level, and a level of specific example. Note this on their student record sheet. Children who are less obvious or verbal in their responses will need to play the game with you individually.

Children whose scores cluster under specific example need many experiences with sorting and classifying concrete objects. This can be a free-time activity played either with you or with a more conceptually advanced buddy.

Children whose scores cluster under functional use simply need to be guided to see that: "Yes, a teacher teaches children. But when we played four square, you taught Mary how to play. You were a teacher too." There is nothing essentially wrong about defining a word according to its function. Adults often do this: "A computer is used to _____ ." We do, however, need to plan Language Experiences that allow children to develop concepts.

Category III: Creative Description

Materials: Stuffed animals, dolls, or puppets; student record sheets

Rather than have the entire class play with the stuffed animals (puppets, dolls) at one time, plan for small groups to play with them. Your goal is to screen out children who do not need individual assessment as well as provide an informal familiarization with the materials. During the play time, ask the children to make up a pretend story with the stuffed animals. You will be listening for a story sequence with a beginning, middle, and an end. You will also be listening to note if any child *consistently* uses incomplete sentences (not occasionally, since we all, in spoken language, use incomplete sentences). Record the information on the student record sheets.

If you are uncertain about a child, plan an individual session. At this time, ask the child to tell you the names of the stuffed animals. Ask the child to tell a pretend story about _____ and _____ . Again, you are listening for a *focused* story sequence. This also indicates whether the child can spontaneously produce complete sentences.

Concluding Thoughts

In assessing oral language production, *you are listening to the content of that production, not the form*. You are listening to the intent of the communication rather than correct usage or pristine articulation. As you are listening to the child, encourage production by responding to what the child means. Do not, under any circumstance, correct the child's language. If you do, you will quite possibly limit if not stop speech production.

This assessment is designed to tell you what children *can do*. The information gained should be used to give you a verbal picture of your children. It is this picture that guides and expands your planning of Language Experience lessons. It should be used as pre-assessment at the beginning of the year and as post-assessment at the end of the year.

Although Assessing Oral Language Production was developed for primary grade (K-3) students, I have used it with learning disabled children and second language learners, and have used a modified form with intermediate grade students. Any students who have not had many opportunities to speak or who have not had many verbal experiences will be identified and their natural abilities developed.

Pertinent Resources

Ashton-Warner, Sylvia. *Teacher*. New York: Bantam, 1964.

Ashton-Warner, Sylvia. *Spearpoint*. New York: Knopf, 1972.

Cazden, Courtney B. *Child Language and Education*. New York: Holt, Rinehart and Winston, 1972.

Hansen-Krening, Nancy. "A Language Acquisition Coding Descriptor of Certain Linguistic Performances." University of Oregon, November, 1974. (Unpublished doctoral dissertation)

Hansen-Krening, Nancy, and Gonzales, Phillip. "Defragmenting Oral Language Instruction and Assessment: A Research Perspective." (An unpublished paper)

Lindfors, Judith. *Children's Language and Learning*. Englewood Cliffs: Prentice-Hall, 1980.

Markova, A. K. *The Teaching and Mastery of Language*. White Plains: M. E. Sharpe, Inc., 1979.

Stauffer, Russell G. *The Language Experience Approach to the Teaching of Reading*. New York: Harper and Row, 1980.

Urzúa, Carole. *Talking Purposefully*. Silver Springs: Institute of Modern Languages, Inc., 1981.

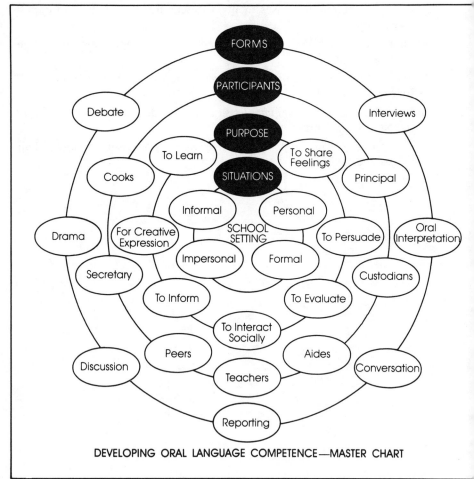

FORMS

PARTICIPANTS

PURPOSE

SITUATIONS

Debate

Interviews

To Learn

To Share
Feelings

Cooks

Principal

Informal

Personal

Drama

For Creative
Expression

SCHOOL
SETTING

To Persuade

Oral
Interpretation

Impersonal

Formal

Secretary

Custodians

To Inform

To Evaluate

To Interact
Socially

Discussion

Peers

Aides

Conversation

Teachers

Reporting

DEVELOPING ORAL LANGUAGE COMPETENCE—MASTER CHART

Developing Oral Language Competence

Children develop control over language use as they extend their out-of-school competence to include in-school, public competence. Students who learn to select form *according to* situation, participants *and* purpose *become powerful communicators.*

Basic Skills:
Beginning and Intermediate Learners

GUIDE FOR "DEVELOPING ORAL LANGUAGE COMPETENCE"
MASTER CHART

Circle 1 *Forms of*
(outside): *Communication*
    Discussion
    Reporting
    Drama
    Oral Interpretation
    Debate
    Interviews
    Conversation

Circle 2: *Communication*
    Participants
    Peers
    Custodians
    Aides
    Principal
    Secretary
    Cooks
    Teachers

Circle 3: *Communication*
    Purpose
    To Evaluate
    To Persuade
    To Share Feelings
    To Learn
    For Creative
      Expression
    To Inform
    To Interact Socially

Circle 4: *Communication*
    Situations
    Formal
    Informal
    Personal
    Impersonal

Inside
Circle: *School Setting*

All students need to consciously work on understanding the roles that situation, participants, and purpose play in selecting the form of their communication. Young children are skilled in this selection process at a tacit level. They know at an unspoken understood level that the forms they choose for oral expression are influenced by those three variables. It is our responsibility to bring that knowledge to the surface. Basic skills remain constant; the ease, creativity, sophistication, and intelligence with which we use them change through practice.

Through listening, speaking, and signing, children exert a direct influence on their environment. The *fluency, ease* and *accuracy* with which they listen and speak directly influences the strength as well as the impact of this contribution. The effectiveness of the contribution relies upon the child's knowledge of the context of the communication, and that means knowing how to use and understand language in different *settings*, with different *purposes*, for varying *audiences*. This is the *communication experience*. For example, if a girl walks into the classroom and whispers, "I don wanna, how come I hafta?" some people would respond with, "What did you say?" The student knew that she wanted to say, "I don't really know what I'm supposed to do. Do I really have to do this?" However, the message could be misunderstood because the girl did not match the form and purpose of her language with the situation and the audience.

The master chart, "Developing Oral Language Competence," (page 20) presents the categories of skills children must master in order to communicate with competence. The category, "Communication Experiences," identifies the primary settings where children experience communication—both school communication and social communication. These are the *settings* in which children will experience oral language and will need to be proficient users of language. Within those settings, the *situations* will vary from formal to informal. Students in a school setting will interact with a variety of familiar and unfamiliar people. The *purposes* of communicating in the context of *situations* and *participants* may be to learn, to evaluate, to persuade, to interact socially, to share feelings, or to express one's self creatively.

The people with whom the student speaks have a great influence on the *form* of the communication. All of the child's past experiences with language determine the technical skill, the fluency, and the accuracy with which he or she communicates. Knowing appropriate language, knowing how to focus—either in speaking or listening—, being able to articulate and use pitch, stress, and juncture—all these are directly tied to the child's knowledge and experience with language. This knowledge must continue to grow and expand as the teacher presents challenges in language learning through the Language Experience Approach. For all children, both first and second language learners, there is the distinct possibility that they will need to learn that different settings, situations, and participants define what is appropriate language and what is acceptable pitch, stress, and juncture. Also, all children will probably have to learn how to focus their speech. For those of us who have stood patiently while children ramble on and on and on with no apparent focus and no apparent end in sight, the necessity of teaching focused talk is obvious.

Using the Master Chart

The master chart may be used as a single resource for teaching basic, oral language proficiency. It may also be used as an organizer in districts that have identified many discrete subskills for oral language proficiency. The master chart may also be used to expand a limited listing of basic skills.

Teachers who approach the teaching of reading and language arts from a holistic viewpoint can use the master chart as a resource for developing language within the context of setting, situation, purpose, and audience.

Regardless of their developmental level and grade level, students must practice developing skills in each category. This requires a shift from elicited (teacher initiated, teacher controlled) talk to spontaneous (open-ended) talk. Elicited talk usually requires limited responses to questions, commands, and modeling. The following illustrates teacher talk which produces elicited speech from the student:

Teacher: *Anna, why do you think Sylvester and his parents put the magic pebble away?*

Anna: *Because they didn't want to waste it.*

Teacher: *Kim, how many eggs did Robin find?*

Kim: *Four.*

Teacher: *Eugenia, what are you supposed to be doing?*

Eugenia: *Paying attention.*

Teacher: *No, Tobias, that is a rack, not a lack. Say rrr-rack.*

Tobias: *Rrr-lack.*

In each of these instances the teacher most certainly has an answer in mind—an expected response from the student. The student knows this and also knows that the response will be evaluated as either right or wrong. In these examples, as in most teacher/student talk, there are constraints on what the student can actually say. All school children participate in elicited speech. Unfortunately for some children, this may be the primary or sole form of teacher/student talk. (Gonzales, Hansen-Krening, 1981) This is particularly true for language-delayed children and for second language learners. Audiolingual language programs that are based on adult/teacher modeling of language provide for elicited responses only.

As teachers, we must realize that, in real life situations, people use language spontaneously. Conversation, for example, is spontaneous talk. Those of us who experience severe difficulty in talking or signing are isolated from human communication. Continuous reluctance to participate in conversations results in a person being labeled as nonverbal, language-delayed, linguistically deficient. Children must develop the power of spontaneous talk; they must be able to initiate talk with others as situations, settings, and participants vary.

Degrees of Oral Language Competence

Children acquire oral language in similar ways. They move through a developmental progression which is quite consistent in all linguistic communities. Children who are learning a second language build on that developmental progression. As with all language learning, they acquire a second language by moving through one-word, two-to-three-word, simple sentences to transformed sentences. Competence for all language learners—in either a first or a second language—will vary with the experiences and abilities of the students. Language-delayed children will, at least initially, progress more slowly than other children. Second language learners, on the other hand, may progress very rapidly—particularly if they are proficient in their first language. The important truth we need to keep in mind is that language competence continues to increase. Ability levels vary, rapidity of growth differs, but if we provide language learning environments, communicative abilities stretch, expand, and grow. Our goal in doing this is to develop the child's existing power in communication, not to deprive the child of this power. Once the student leaves school, new settings, situations, participants, purposes, and audiences will consistently and continuously push that growth even further.

Organization of Language Experience Lessons

The language experience activities are organized holistically. That is, each activity provides practice with a combination of oral language skills within the total communication experience. However, each activity will emphasize specific skills. It will also identify the focus of the activity. There will be a set of lessons labeled "Survival Language." These are designed to develop a basic level of oral language proficiency, a level required for survival in school and in the community.

The master chart identifies settings for the communication experience; the oral language lessons in this text will take place in one setting, the school. But through role playing, children will practice using oral language in different situations with different participant settings that would exist out of school. Some of these lessons can be used to involve the parents or the primary caretakers in the child's development of oral language skills.

Second language learners should begin these lessons according to their developmental levels. If they are monolingual in a language other than English, they must begin with survival language. Once they become proficient enough to communicate using survival language, the students may move on to the beginning activities. Progress through these language experiences should be paced according to the abilities of the student. Some students may need extended oral language interaction while others may not.

Children with special needs, hearing impaired children would begin, according to their proficiency in either oral language or sign language, at either beginning or intermediate levels.

If the child uses sign language, you probably will need an interpreter or an aide in decoding the message. The resource person and the child can also teach you and your class as much sign language as is functional as well as practicable. Although there are books that teach signing, they are as limited in use as are books that teach spoken speech without human resources.

And do keep in mind, regardless of any constraints or limitations of time, oral reading and story telling are integral parts of any language learning environment. You must read to your class or tell stories to your class every single day.

Language Experience Lessons: Beginning Learners

LESSON 1: Conversation

All children like to talk about things directly related to their own lives. In developing conversation, you cannot simply say, "Talk to each other." If you do, the children probably won't know where to begin. You can initiate conversation by giving it some direction. One way of doing this is to read a book such as *Crow Boy* (Taro Yashima. New York: Puffin Paperback, 1976). *Crow Boy* tells of the agony of being shy and frightened in a school setting. After reading the story to the class, ask the children to talk about their feelings when they came to school on the first day. Once the talk flows, say something like, "You all have interesting stories, but since there are so many of us, I would like you to sit with someone in the room and tell them about your feelings when you came to school. That way everyone will have a chance to talk, and everyone will have a chance to listen." The children may separate into small groups or sets of two and simply talk with each other.

LESSON 2: Conversation

The teacher may follow the first activity by having children talk about the feelings of other people. They may use recorded tapes of people talking. These voices should reflect different emotions such as excitement, happiness, sadness, and anger. The children may discuss their interpretations of the feelings expressed by the voices. A tape recorder may be placed in a quiet spot in the room where the children may go and record their own voices as they express different emotions. The class may listen to those recordings and talk about their interpretations of the feelings they hear in the voices.

LESSON 3: Conversation—Situational Change

An ideal beginning for this lesson would be for the teacher to play a pre-recorded tape. This tape would include the verbal and nonverbal sounds from the playground, from the lunchroom, from directed lessons in class, and from people talking in a formal situation (such as in a conference with the principal). After listening to the entire tape, the children could listen to individual segments and talk about the sounds of language. The teacher could lead the group conversation by asking questions such as, "Listen to the voices. How do they sound to you?" "Where do you think these children are?" "What do you think they might be doing?" "Why are they talking this way?" The questions should be used as an initial focus only.

After listening to and talking about the voices, the teacher may ask the children if their own voices are always the same: if they always talk the same way to everyone. (For example, many young children love to shout on the playground, "Blue, blue, you've got the flu, no one wants to play with you!" If anyone shouted this chant in the classroom, the children would be shocked.) The teacher may focus on this contrast between playground language and classroom language. The contrast would include appropriate language, tone of voice, and clarity of speech: when and where are these important? The class could then identify different conversational situations in which they talk with different people (parents, brothers and sisters, adults, friends, clerks in stores, bus drivers). The children should identify the tone of voice and language they would use in talking with different people in different situations. During their free time children may wish to choose partners with whom they can tape record pretend conversations with different people. They will need to shape their voices and their language to fit both the situation and the people who are talking. Some children may wish to role play these conversations in front of the rest of the class. The class members would have to guess the situation and the participants by listening to the voices and the spoken language.

LESSON 4: Discussion—Solving Problems

Children often argue over who gets to take out the playground equipment and who was first in line. The teacher may use these or similar topics to introduce spontaneous discussion. For example: "I have noticed that every time we go out for recess, some of you always want to be first in line. I think this is a problem because your voices are loud and you argue. Let's take time to talk about who should be first in line. When you tell who you think should be first, I want you to tell *why*. *Why* should that person be first?" The "why" aspect of a discussion is important. In a discussion, reasons for opinions and attitudes must be given. Additionally, the teacher should remind the children that tone of voice and clearness in speaking are important if they want people to listen to them, to understand them. An extension of this lesson would be continued class discussion on other decision-making situations such as: "What shall we do in P.E.?" "What songs would you like to learn?" "Who should get to use the paints?" "Who should be the class leader?"

LESSON 5: Reporting—Informal

Children enjoy responsibility that implies they are grown-up. Every year there are occasions the teacher might use to develop oral reporting skills. For example: if a field trip is being planned; if a guest speaker is being invited to the classroom; if a party is being planned; if another classroom is being invited in to see a play. In each case, there are procedures that must be followed. There may be permission slips to be handed out, buses to be ordered, the principal to talk with, the speaker to be called— any one of a number of steps to be followed to achieve a specific goal. The class can identify those procedures; volunteers may query sources of information; and, finally, reports to the class may be made. If adults or other classrooms are involved in the activity, the class may need to decide how to persuade that adult or class to participate. Whatever the ultimate goal, the procedure should follow this organization:

1. What is the goal? What do we want to do?
2. Who and what are involved? What will we have to do to get ready?
3. How will we convince people to participate?
4. Who will do the talking?
5. When should we be finished? When should classmates report back to class?
6. After the reports, will we still have things to do? What are they?

LESSON 6: Interviewing

This activity should be combined with the preceding activity. If children are to talk with other adults such as prospective speakers, other teachers, or the principal, they need to practice or role play interviewing procedures. What is appropriate language? What is appropriate tone of voice? How will they stick to the topic? These questions should be discussed before the interviews take place. When the children report back to the class, they can evaluate their own success in talking with the adults.

LESSON 7: Persuading

Speaking persuasively to an audience of peers is a sophisticated skill. It requires that the speaker understand the viewpoint of the audience. For young children this is not always possible. For children who are more advanced developmentally, it is a positive challenge. The teacher might start by saying something like, "Are there times when you try to get someone to do something that *you* want to do? Are their times when you try to talk someone into doing something?" The children should be given time to respond to these questions. The next step is for the teacher to ask why we try to talk people into doing something. For example, we might need to convince a little brother or sister to go to bed, to eat supper or to get a vaccination. These are instances where we want people to do things that will help them. When we are doing this, we must think of reasons the person will understand. After discussing possible reasons that will persuade people, the teacher may work with the class on a specific topic, such as: to get someone to eat a hot lunch; to wash their hands; to get more sleep; to get to school on time—any topic that is meaningful in the daily lives of the children.

An extension of this activity is for an individual or small groups of children to plan a persuasive talk. This talk could be to convince the class to eat a favorite food, watch a favorite television show, or play a favorite game.

LESSON 8: Debate

This activity is a natural extension of the preceding one. Children can debate about which food is best; which television shows are best; whether or not children should go to school, have vaccinations, eat hot lunch. . . . This is a fledgling debate, and it will require that they use all the skills they have been practicing in the other oral language experiences.

Lessons on creative dramatics and oral interpretation can be found in *Competency and Creativity in Language Arts* (Hansen-Krening. Reading, MA: Addison-Wesley, 1979).

Out of School Communication Experiences

Teachers write newsletters to parents as a means of stimulating out-of-school oral communication experiences. In writing the newsletter, it is important to keep several things in mind. The teacher must use language that avoids educational jargon. If the parents are monolingual in a language other than English, or if their English is not as firm as their first language, the teacher must find a resource person to write the newsletter in the parents' first language. The resource person may be a student, an aide, a volunteer from the community, or a member of district bilingual personnel. Before sending the letter home, the teacher should be sure the child's culture encourages children speaking on an informal basis with parents or primary caretakers. Furthermore, the conversation should not focus on the child's "bragging" about what the child has done in school. There are cultures that value modesty and humility.

Suggestions for Oral Language Development in the Home

The teacher could suggest that the parent or primary caretaker talk with the child about:

1. The teachers and other adults in the school.
2. What the child is learning about using language with others. The teacher could include a description of the oral language activities being used in the classroom.
3. The child's best friend at school.
4. The names of objects in the home and community. This is a valuable technique for expanding the child's oral language vocabulary.
5. What the child is reading in school.
6. What the child likes to play on the playground.

In addition to this, the newsletters should consistently encourage parents to read to their children. If parents allot even five minutes of communication each day, alone with each child, it would be a boon for that child's oral language development. Reading aloud from both fiction and nonfiction is an absolute must for all children, regardless of age.

Language Experience Lessons: Intermediate Learners

Students should always be told the purpose of whatever they are doing. They should understand the intent of the lesson. By knowing *why* they are doing what they are doing, students will be able to generalize and to apply the skills being learned to situations where those skills are needed. They will conceptualize rather than memorize.

The teacher should introduce lessons on oral language with an explanation of the need for competence in speaking and listening. Much of our time is spent listening. We listen to receive news, opinions, directions, attitudes, ideas; we listen to maintain contact with the world. All of us need to learn to listen with comprehension. We need to remember facts. ("What did he say his telephone number is?") We need to listen to infer meaning from what we hear. ("Why do you think she said that to me?") We need to listen to, and to critically assess, information we receive from the media. ("What are they really trying to sell? What are the hidden meanings?") Perceptive listening is powerful listening; it is listening for autonomous decision-making.

Speech is one of the most obvious projections of ourselves. Through the telephone and through recordings, the human voice and the message it carries transcends time and space. The skill with which we communicate impresses people with an image of our ability to express ourselves fluently and proficiently. A person who is fluent and proficient transmits information accurately and, consequently, avoids having to constantly repeat what has been said. That person also avoids confusion in interpersonal, social, and school communication. Speaking proficiently gives power to the speaker.

LESSON 1: Conversation

Initial experiences with classroom conversation often need some direction. Students may feel self-conscious or uncomfortable in a school setting using a conversational form. There are several directions the first language experiences could take. If there are enough students in the classroom, the teacher can form several small conversational groups. The members of the group can talk with any new students, explaining school and class routines and answering questions. Another approach to conversation is putting the students in sets of two, one person designated as talker, one as listener. While the talker is talking, the listener may not interrupt. After three to five minutes, the teacher signals the class to stop talking; at another signal, the listener becomes the talker and must paraphrase what he has just heard from his partner. The teacher should plan to repeat these conversational experiences until the teacher has had an opportunity to listen, informally, to every conversation. Naturally, this listening should be as unobtrusive as possible, or it will place constraints on the oral language of the students. By listening to students talk in these peer conversations, the teacher has an initial assessment of each student's oral language proficiency.

LESSON 2: Conversation

You may suggest topics of conversation such as: How do you feel about school? Do you feel that school is necessary? If you could change this school, what would you change? These questions focus on feelings but avoid intruding on the students' personal feelings about themselves. The students may begin talking as a large group and then quickly split into smaller groups.

LESSON 3: Conversation—Situational Change

Begin by playing a tape recording of teachers' voices. The voices should first identify the participants and then move into slang-filled conversation. Since slang phrases change almost by the second, the recorded phrases should be as current as possible. The scenario might be similar to this:

Teacher 1: *Good morning, Ms. _____ .* (Insert principal's name.)

Principal: *Good morning, Mr. _____ .* (Insert teacher's name.)

Teacher 2: *Do you plan to have a fire drill today, Ms. _____ ?*

Principal: *I hadn't anticipated doing so.*

Teacher 2: *Is there some reason for your not doing so?*

Principal: *Yeah, those turkey kids'll just freak out.*

Teacher 1: *Say, girl, my kids're spaced now. I don't need that kind of action!*

Teacher 2: *For sure! I've got a room full of space cadets already!*

Principal: *Later.*

Teachers 1 and 2: *Yeah, later.*

After the tape has been played, the class can talk about their reactions to the talk they heard. Did they expect the teachers and the principal to use the kind of language they did? The students should be asked if they use the same kind of language with all people. As the class conversation proceeds, the teacher should (if the students do not) introduce the specific idea of "code-switching;" that is, changing language according to the situation and the participants. The class can talk about situations where they code-switch. Finally, students may role play in a series of conversational code-switching situations with a variety of participants. The rest of the class must identify both the situation where and the participants for whom the language is appropriate.

The second part of this activity focuses on the use of tone of voice, stress, and juncture. You may introduce this part of the lesson by saying, "CLASS, what are you doing?" "Class, what ARE you doing?" "Class, WHAT—ARE—YOU—DOING?" "C-L-A-S-S, what are Y-O-U-doing?" The class should discuss the way the message was changed by the tone of voice, emphasis of words, and the use of pauses. As a class, the students can identify phrases that can be altered by the use of pitch, stress, and juncture. Small groups of students may then write phrases on slips of paper. These papers may be exchanged with other groups of students. Each group should practice saying the phrases with as many combinations of articulation, tone of voice, stress, and pause as they can. As a follow-up to this lesson, students should listen to out-of-school language and determine how talk is made more interesting, as well as more accurate, by using technical skills. They can also learn how writers represent vocal changes by altering the size and shape of print.

LESSON 4: Discussion—Informal

The class should be reminded that group discussion requires: active listening, giving reasons for stated opinions; encouraging others to speak; keeping contributions focused on the topic; and speaking clearly with appropriate pitch, stress, and juncture.

Divide the class into groups of eight to ten students. Each of these groups should be split into subgroups A and B. Through discussion, subgroup A must convince subgroup B that it should do all of subgroup A's homework for a week. Subgroup B must then, through persuasive discussion, try to change the minds of subgroup A. This lesson may be extended by shifting topics and changing groups. Other topics for discussion might include: should girls be allowed to participate in school sports; should schools be changed to all-girl schools and all-boy schools; men should accept more responsibility for helping in the home; or any other topic that would stimulate the interest and language of the class.

LESSON 5: Reporting

There are many topics that lend themselves to spontaneous reporting. For example, the class may list subjects such as:

1. Adding more interesting books to the school library.
2. Adding movie magazines, television magazines, and comic books to the school or class library.
3. Adding rock records to the school or class music collection.
4. Giving students more (or less) power in decision-making at school.
5. Allowing students to choose the schools they want to attend.
6. Allowing students to choose their teachers.

Class members choose a topic they find interesting. They then talk with students from other classes and ask them what books, magazines, and records they would add to the school's existing collections.

They could determine which school policies are the most controversial. After talking with other students, each class member reports back to the class. These reports would be informal class reports on the results of their investigations.

LESSON 6: Interview

As an extension of the last activity, students interview teachers, the principal, the person in charge of the library, and other school personnel. The interviews would elicit adult views on the topics the students reported on in the last language experience activity. Before the interviews, students may role play, practicing their interview techniques and language. The actual interviews can be tape recorded, played for the class, and evaluated for effective and proficient use of oral language. As a final step the students write reports (perhaps in the form of a newspaper) to share with the school.

LESSON 7: Persuading

Critical thinking is essential in a consumer-oriented society. Students need to know how language is used to sell products and influence decision-making. In this activity, students are asked to listen to the radio, watch television, and read advertisements. Students identify the words and phrases used to persuade people to buy different products, and report their investigations to the class. At this time, list examples of persuasive language on chart paper. These lists may be used by the students in making their own commercials for either real or imagined products. These commercials are then presented to the rest of the class through video tapes (simulated commercials), simulated radio broadcasts, and role-played television or radio broadcasts. The class can then express their views on truth in advertising, the ethics of advertising, and controls on advertising which should or should not be set.

LESSON 8: Debate

The debate topic may be drawn from any of the last three activities. Doing so would provide a natural, developmental flow in gathering information, reporting on that information, and debating the negative and positive aspects of that information. For example, if the topic is whether or not students want comic books in school, the students would have assessed student and teacher opinions and would have evaluated the strengths and weaknesses of these opinions. After determining their own positions, debates could take place. Students should have ample time to organize their information and practice their oral presentations. The audience should award points to the debaters on the basis of accurate information, effective presentation, and proficient use of oral language.

Lessons on creative dramatics and oral interpretation can be found in *Competency and Creativity in Language Arts* (Hansen-Krening. Reading, MA: Addison-Wesley, 1979).

Additional Ideas

At the intermediate level, students should be able to go into the business community and talk with workers, business people and service people. Class members may ask these people about the ways in which they must use language. Are there certain words or phrases that relate to specific professions? Are there appropriate and inappropriate languages for different jobs? If it is possible, students may tape record these conversations and share them with the class. Students may report back to the class.

Students may speak with their parents, primary caretakers, grandparents, aunts and uncles. They may ask these people if language has changed since they were children; if they think language should change; about their attitudes toward speaking; do they think conversation is important? Do they like to talk? What do they like to talk about, avoid talking about? With whom do they like to talk? Why do they have the attitudes and opinions they have?

Students could listen to the oral language of small children and compare it with that of older children. How does oral language change as people grow older?

The class may invite bilingual teachers or resource people to visit the class to speak about their own out-of-school experiences in learning a new language; or they may speak about similarities and differences in languages, differences in the uses of language, and cultural differences reflected in language. The resource people could speak about appropriate form in their first language compared with appropriate form in their second language, and about language differences in using pitch, stress, and juncture.

The teacher should use all of these experiences to consistently emphasize the flexible nature of oral language, and the fact that oral language can be mastered and used by students (rather than the students being restricted by language). *Oral language gives us control over our own lives.*

Survival Language:
Non-English Speaking Children

When monolingual, non-English speaking children enter school, it is imperative that they learn survival language immediately! Common sense should dictate what the nature of that language should be. At first, survival language will be one- or two-word expressions. These expressions or words should be taught *in context*. For instance, students should be at the door of the restroom when they learn the word *restroom*. The emphasis is on learning the appropriate label. Precise articulation can be developed much later; survival language is concerned only with speaking clearly enough to be understood.

Some words and phrases that should be taught first are: *restroom, food, water, book, paper, class, walk, bus, recess, lunch, school, mother, father, home, desk, pencil, telephone, friend, yes, no,* and *teacher*. The student should also learn to say, "I don't understand," and "My name is—," and should learn the teacher's name, the name of the school, the student's home address and telephone number, the name of her parents or primary caretaker, and the name of the family doctor, if there is one.

Peer group teaching is invaluable in learning a second language. Peers are in closer, more intimate contact with the monolingual, non-English speaking child than the teacher and are often less threatening than an adult. By assigning a buddy or buddies to the new child, the teacher is assuring that there will be a steady learning of a second language.

Survival language extends from school survival into community survival language. The teacher and the buddies should help the child learn labels for experiences that are likely to occur outside of school. By going for walks or riding the bus home, the monolingual, non-English speaking child can learn *grocery store, street, sidewalk, walk, wait, drugstore, gas station, telephone booth,* and *building*. They also may learn the meaning of such phrases as, "May I help you?" "What do you want?" "Where do you live?" "You owe me. . . ."

Survival Language Lessons

In teaching survival language, the teacher should speak to the child in simple, yet complete, sentences. Repetition should focus on the key words. You may want to use a limited amount of different word combinations, which allow the child to hear the key word in a variety of *contexts*, just as the key word will be heard in actual conversation. This approach most closely parallels the language experiences the child will encounter in school, as well as in the community. Survival language must be taught using concrete experiences in context.

LESSON 1

Take the child to the restroom, point to the door and say, "This is the *restroom.*" Take the child inside and say, "The *restroom* has sinks and toilets." Go to the sink and show the child that this is for washing hands saying, "I wash my hands in the *restroom.*" Point to the urinal and/or the stall and show the child how they flush. Say, "Toilets are in the *restroom.*" If buddies are used to show the child the restroom, role play or carefully explain the language experience to the child. The buddy-teacher or peer-teacher must use the word *restroom* because that is the public survival term. Teaching slang would only result in possible embarrassment to the second language learner.

LESSON 2

Follow the same basic procedure as above, for teaching the student where to get a drink of water.

LESSON 3

Follow the same basic procedure for teaching where to go for lunch.

LESSON 4

Follow the same basic procedure for teaching how to find the class-room.

LESSON 5

Follow the same procedure for teaching how to find the bus stop.

In these initial activities, the child should not be expected to use complete sentences. The lessons are successful if the child first learns, in the listening vocabulary, to understand (and later say) the words *restroom, drink, classroom,* and *lunch.* When the child is able to speak these single words as they are needed or as they are appropriate, a major step in learning has occurred. The child has begun to acquire and conceptualize English as a second language.

Once the language for physical survival is acquired, children should learn to say, "I don't understand," and "yes," and "no." Since these are more abstract concepts, the teacher might have difficulty providing a concrete language experience in English. Consequently, the teacher—not the child—should learn to say, "Do you understand?" "I don't understand," "Yes," "No," "Show me," and "Do you need help?" in the child's first language. If there are as many as five or six languages represented in the classroom, the teacher should learn these phrases and words in all five or six languages. The words and phrases should be learned as quickly as possible for several reasons. For example, in most classrooms a smile and a nod means, "I understand." However, in another culture, this same nonverbal behavioral combination is no more than a standard response children give when listening to adults. It does not indicate understanding but is a polite, courteous, expected behavior. Confusion and misunderstanding for both the teacher and the child could develop unless the teacher learns to say, "Do you understand?" and also learns to pause and listen for the child's answer.

As a resource, I have asked individuals at the Bilingual Resource Center in Seattle, Washington to write those phrases for your use. Since some languages are tonal, they do not allow for phonetic spelling. Not all phrases are spelled phonetically.

DO YOU UNDERSTAND?

Japanese: *Wakarimasu ka?*
(standard spelling)
Wakárĕmas ka?
(phonetic spelling)

Korean: *Ah-see-et-sum-ni-ka?*
(phonetic spelling)

Spanish: *¿Comprende?*
(standard spelling)
cōm prĕń dă

Vietnamese: *Em/chi có hiêủ k' hông?*
(standard spelling)

Mandarin: *Niń ming bai ma?*

Cantonese: *Néih jì-dou ngóh góng māt-yeh ma?*

I DON'T UNDERSTAND.

Japanese: *Wakarimasen*
(standard spelling)

Wakarĭmasen
(phonetic spelling)

Korean: *Moul-a-yo*
(phonetic spelling)

Spanish: *No comprendo*
(standard spelling)
No cōm prĕń dō
(phonetic spelling)

Vietnamese: *Tôi không hiêủ*
(standard spelling)

Mandarin: *Wŏ bu ming bai*
(standard spelling)

Cantonese: *Nḡoh m̀h j̀i-dou*

YES

Japanese: *Hai*
(standard spelling)
Hi
(phonetic spelling)

Korean: *Nae*
(phonetic spelling)

Spanish: *Sí*
(standard spelling)
See
(phonetic spelling)

Vietnamese: *có*
(standard spelling)

Cantonese: *Hai*
(standard spelling)

NO

Japanese: *Iie*
(standard spelling)
ĕyĕh
(phonetic spelling)

Korean: *Ah-nie-yo*
(phonetic spelling)

Spanish: *No*
(standard and phonetic spelling)

Vietnamese: *khong*
(standard spelling)

Cantonese: *m̀-haih*

SHOW ME.

Japanese: *misete kudasai*
(standard spelling)
mǐ sě tě kǔ dǎ sǎ ǐ
(phonetic spelling)

Korean: *Bo-yo-ju-sae-yo*
(phonetic spelling)

Spanish: *Muestreme*
(standard spelling)
mueś tray may
(phonetic spelling)

Vietnamese: *chi cho toi*
(standard spelling)

Mandarin: *Gei wo kan*

DO YOU NEED HELP?

Japanese: *Tetsudate agemashoo ka?*
(standard spelling)
tět sǔ dǎt tě ǎgě mǎ show kǎ
(phonetic spelling)

Korean: *Dom-ie peel-yo-ha-sae-yo?*
(phonetic spelling)

Spanish: *Necesita ayuda?*
(standard spelling)
Ně sě sē´ tǎ ī yoo dǎ?
(phonetic spelling)

Vietnamese: *Em/chi/em có cân guiṗ gī không?*
(standard spelling)

Mandarin: *Nin shi yau bang mang*[1]

Additional resources for the language-learning teacher:

1. Other students who are bilingual in both the child's first language and in American English.
2. Parents, aunts, uncles, and grandparents.
3. People in the community who are bilingual in the child's first language and in American English.
4. Bilingual resource people in the school district.
5. Language-learning phonograph recordings or tapes in the school, town, college, or county libraries (if all else fails).

---

[1] I thank Daisy Lu, Ogi Ahn, Lily Woo, Carlos Cardona Morales, Xuyen Ngo, and most especially Diane Collum for help with these phrases.

Students may learn words and phrases (such as *pencil, book, paper, friend, sit down, go out for recess, get ready*) in the same way they learned initial survival language.

Although specific words and phrases have been presented in these survival language activities, the individual teacher is the only person who can identify and prioritize the words and phrases that need to be learned. The language of the individual classroom is the survival language for the student.

If the teacher and the class simply would envision themselves in a country where no one spoke their first language, it would be relatively easy to decide what second language learners need to know. It would also be easier to understand why precise articulation of new words is not as important as simply being clear enough to be understood. Nothing will inhibit initial language learning more than being over-corrected.

Developing Oral Language in Hearing Impaired Children

Hearing impairment affects the ease with which children acquire oral language skills. It does not eliminate the ability to develop some proficiency in oral language. Since hearing is a facilitator in learning labels for new and old experiences, and since learning the sound combinations which produce those labels involves hearing, the hearing impaired child may require closer contact with the teacher in the beginning oral language activities.

The intimate nature of Language Experience and the continuing, close contact between students and teacher is particularly beneficial for hearing impaired children. For the child who uses oral language and speech-reading as primary communication channels, the teacher can sit or kneel close by the child's face. The child may also touch the teacher's face as the teacher speaks. This is accomplished easily and inconspicuously since initial activities may be based on small-group or one-to-one situations. In these activities the students communicate informally or spontaneously. The child (as do all children) becomes accustomed to communicating first in nonthreatening situations. Communicating in larger, more formal situations comes toward the end of a developmental sequence.

Aids for the Hearing Impaired Child

Hearing impairment varies as much in degree of hearing loss as it does in causes and recency of loss. The degree of loss in children ranges from slight loss in one ear to profound loss in both ears. The causes may vary from prenatal to recent accidental loss. Children who were born deaf are congenitally deaf; children who become deaf before language skills were acquired are pre-lingually deaf; children who become deaf after acquiring language are post-lingually deaf. These labels are just that, labels. They are important only in understanding the nature of the loss and its effects on oral language learning.

Following the diagnosis and the assessment of the degree of hearing loss, children are, ideally, fitted with hearing aids.

> A child may be fitted with one hearing aid with a single cord, but with a mold for each ear for alternate use. In some cases, one hearing aid with Y cord arrangement and a receiver for each ear may be deemed more suitable. More and more frequently, two hearing aids (one for each ear) are being recommended, even for infants. (Harris, Grace. *Language for the Preschool Deaf Child.* New York: Grune and Stratton, 1971.)

As a rule, the earlier the child is fitted with a hearing aid, the better. Hearing aids often help younger children acquire oral language early. Further assistance for hearing impaired children is provided by experience-based preschools for the hearing impaired. Children who have entered these programs while still quite young have usually had their intellectual development and language learning nurtured. Parents are often closely involved in these preschool programs so that there is sustained learning between home and school. There are, of course, parents who bring their children to the school as a further step in their own, parent-oriented, language-rich planning for the child.

Oral Language, Manual Alphabet, Sign Language, and Language Experience

Hearing impaired people may communicate through a variety of channels: oral language, which is speaking (expressive) and speech or lip reading (receptive); manual alphabet (the less commonly used finger spelling of words); sign language (using manual language to represent concepts and ideas); simultaneous communication (using both oral communication and signing); and total communication which includes speech, speech reading, signing, finger spelling, body language, and reading and writing.

The Education for All Handicapped Children Act, P.L.94-142, insures that the classroom teacher will know which of the preceding methods have been used in teaching communication skills to the child. The form of the child's communication is not the key factor—that the child *does* communicate is the key factor. Whether the child uses oral language, sign language, simultaneous communication, or total communication, the language experience progression will remain the same. The only difference lies in the initial mode. The child may speak a sentence or sign it; in either case, the teacher will respond to the message, not to the medium. Later, when the child is dictating stories, the teacher's response will be to record, with printed symbols, what the child has expressed. The child will see the relationship between the signed word and words in print.

The oral language activities in this chapter should provide the sequence of oral language activities for the hearing impaired child. Regardless of the language used, the demands on oral proficiency remain the same. Using different forms, the child must learn to communicate in different settings and different situations, with different purposes, and for differing audiences. These language experiences are designed to develop accuracy and fluency in both the senders and receivers of the messages.

Evaluating Oral Language Competence

Oral language proficiency can only be assessed in actual performance. Furthermore, *that performance should be in the context where the skill is needed*. Each of the activities in this chapter is planned to develop oral language proficiency in context. As each activity involves student language, the teacher should evaluate, assess, and record pupil language performance. The teacher may use a record-keeping code used by the school district, or use a code that indicates: I (improving); A (adequate progress); N (needs more work); P (proficient). If records are kept for each activity, the teacher has a complete record for each child, specifying language experience and the performance of the child in that activity. The record will be available for use in filling out report cards as well as for parent/teacher and teacher/pupil conferencing. A steady progression through the suggested activities of the Language Experience Approach provides development of all the oral language skills that have been designated as basic skills in developing oral language competence.

Another resource for evaluating oral language competence is through developing an Informal Oral Language Inventory. Assessment is informal and occurs within the context of situation, purpose, and form. I have used an Informal Inventory in several classes while I was teaching the entire class. It is easy to use and more accurate than

LEVEL II		
General descriptors: Use in many situations and with many individuals	Function	

SCHOOL		SOCIAL	
Labels, identifies, classifies information		Gives directions for games	
Can tell when they don't understand		Expands social contacts (aides, teachers, and peers)	
Recalls at literal level		Enjoys telling how and what of personal experiences	
Can understand directions with one or two variables at a time			
Needs directions verbalized		**LINGUISTIC**	
Language experience possible		Uses simple sentences	
Asks for repeated information		Conjunctions: and, but, or, because, so, as	
Can participate in simple, literal: discussions, reporting, drama, interviews		Present progressive (-ing verbs)	
Responds to elicited talk		Formulates and answers questions: who, what, which, where	
		Simple future (going to . . .)	
GENERAL		Irregular plurals	
Expands pat phrases		Past tense is inadequately developed	
Actively constructs sentences			
Understands similarities and differences			
Literal comprehension			

most assessment tools. The format is a checklist; all you need do is listen to children use their language in different situations, for different purposes, with different participants, using different forms. As you listen, you check off the dominant characteristics of the child's oral language. The result is a profile of the child's oral language competence. The above is a sample page from such an inventory.

Concluding Thoughts

Our aural receptive and expressive powers are being used constantly. This demand as well as the need to communicate encompasses a range of situations, purposes, participants and forms. In order to be in control (rather than be controlled) during these communication acts, we must have a comprehensive repertoire of aural language skills. The person who remains quiet out of fear or embarrassment is not in control. I think all of us have experienced that feeling of intimidation. We have been in situations when we wanted to say something but have not simply because we were afraid of sounding foolish or ignorant. In those instances we were powerless, a frustrating feeling. Teaching children to recognize the need to suit their aural communication skills to the setting, situation, purpose, and participants reduces the likelihood of their feeling inadequate.

If you analyze the master chart, Developing Oral Language Competence, you might feel that it is unnecessary for all of your students to develop competence in, for instance, oral interpretation, and drama. I believe that is not true. It would be wrong to sacrifice any student's opportunity for creative expression. Every person needs to be able to both receive and express with creativity. *Competency and Creativity in Language Arts* (Hansen-Krening, N. Reading, MA: Addison-Wesley, 1979); *Literature for Thursday's Child* (Sebesta, S. and W. Iverson, C. Chicago: SRA, 1975); *Creative Drama in the Elementary School* (McIntyre, B. Itasca: Peacock Publishers, 1974); and *Drama With Children* (Siks, G. New York: Harper and Row, 1977) provide highly practical ideas for developing creative expression.

Finally, read to your students every day. Children must hear language in its many varieties. Plan to read folk tales, realistic fiction, fantasy and nonfiction. Read from encyclopedias. Read from social studies and science texts. Informal sharing of nonfiction in a story time setting models a valuing of nonfiction while also stimulating an interest in these valuable resources.

Pertinent Resources

Bornstein, Harry; Lillian B. Hamilton; Karen Luczak Saulnier; Howard L. Roy. *The Signed English Dictionary for Preschool and Elementary Levels.* Washington D.C.: Gallaudet College Press, 1975.

Fant, Louie J., Jr. *Ameslan.* Northridge, CA: Joyce Motion Picture Co., 1977.

Hansen-Krening, N. and P. G. Gonzales. "Assessing the Language Learning Environment in Classrooms." *Educational Leadership*, March, 1981.

Hansen-Krening, Nancy. *Competency and Creativity in Language Arts: A Multiethnic Focus.* Reading, MA: Addison-Wesley, 1979.

Harris, Grace M. *Language for the Preschool Deaf Child*, 3rd edition. New York: Grune and Stratton, 1971.

Lindfors, Judith Wells. *Children's Language and Learning.* Englewood Cliffs: Prentice-Hall, 1980.

Playing with Words: Metalinguistic Awareness

Basic Skills: Beginning Learners

The student will:

- learn the relationship between spoken words and words in print and associate this relationship with decoding words in print.
- learn the purpose of the mechanics of manuscript (printing).
- learn the purpose of spelling.
- learn that sentences convey meaning, and relate this to sentence forms.
- learn to identify what a word is, both in speaking and in print.
- learn the purpose and use of capitalization.
- learn the purpose and use of punctuation.
- develop beginning comprehension skills.
- develop left to right sequencing.
- learn that people share oral traditions—regardless of ethnic membership or first language.
- learn that this oral tradition often has common form.
- develop attitudes of sharing and cooperation through group work.

Basic Skills: Intermediate Learners

The student will learn:

the purpose of word recognition skills.

the different purposes of and uses of comprehension skills.

the purposes of different forms of composition.

the purpose of editing and proofreading.

the purpose of the mechanics of cursive writing.

the purpose of standard spelling.

the purpose of using complete sentences.

the purposes of different forms of punctuation.

that people share oral traditions—regardless of ethnic membership or first language.

that this oral tradition often has common form.

to develop attitudes of sharing and cooperation through group work.

Research contributes at least two things to the teaching profession: valuable new knowledge or confirmation of existing knowledge, and incomprehensible jargon.

At first glance, the phrase *metalinguistic awareness* seems to be a perfect example of incomprehensible jargon. And it may be—but it is also a phrase that represents an invaluable body of information garnered from research.

Metalinguistic awareness frees us to look at language as something apart from ourselves. It facilitates the realization that language is a tool every individual can use; that language is an entity shaped and controlled by individuals. Metalinguistic awareness precedes developing competency in reading and language arts.

For example, in order to understand the purpose and function of phonics skills, children must first understand that words in print are no more than just that—words in print. As speech uses sound to communicate ideas, words in print use visual symbols to present those same ideas. Sound (unless captured by tape) is fleeting, while print remains more or less permanent. The immediate, yet transitory, nature of speech may impede our conscious awareness of language as something we create. In order to understand that words are arbitrary symbols, we must learn to disassociate ourselves from language. We must, in a sense, be able to stand back and look at language objectively, as a thing apart from ourselves.

Metalinguistic awareness anticipates the child's ability to understand the purpose for and development of the basic skills involved in learning to apply inferential, critical, and creative comprehension skills in listening, speaking, reading, and writing. It is of particular importance in understanding the relationship between phonics skills and reading. By being consciously aware of our control over our language, we can understand that words can both be taken apart *and* put together again (decoding and encoding). We can also know the *purpose* of: word recognition skills; punctuation, capitalization; standard spelling; the use of a variety of forms in composition; standard usage, and the different sentence forms. Students who develop metalinguistic awareness see the utility, the purpose, of basic skill mastery. Without this *knowing* of the reason why, student learning objectives are meaningless hoops that teachers must hold while their students jump, stumble, or fall through.

Playing with Words: Metalinguistic Awareness begins the deliberate development of metalinguistic awareness. At this step in the Language Experience Approach, teachers are responsible for helping students make the transition from spoken language to language in print.

This transitional step, from oral language to language in print, is pivotal because it develops metalinguistic awareness while also developing reading readiness. At this step, children actually watch the almost simultaneous, written transcription of their own spoken language. The child watches the person take dictation and record exactly what the child has said almost as quickly as it is said. Children literally see their spoken words take printed form. The child chants, "When I was one. . ." as teacher says, "I'm going to write the words you said." As the child watches, the teacher says each dictated word while writing, "When–I–was–one. . ."

Through dictating chants, riddles, and jokes, children learn to see words as sets of individual letters, and sentences as sets of individual words. They see that the words in print follow a consistent left to right sequence. This dictation also facilitates the development of the meaning for parts of speech because children see the concrete referents for terms such as: sentence, word, subject, verb, and object.

Through viewing oral language taking shape in print, children watch as the teacher models the correct formation of letters. They learn the left to right sequencing of reading and writing. They see the use and purpose of capital letters, periods, and commas. Through dictating they learn the names of letters as those letters spell words. Children also learn that they can control their own expression by adding or deleting words. They even learn that printed words can be erased!

The person taking dictation must consistently point out exactly what she is doing:

"You said, 'Juba this, Juba that. . .' This is the word, 'Juba.'"

"I always start a sentence with a capital letter. You said, 'What is yellow and goes click, click?' I am making a capital W for the word, 'What.'"

"You know, in math we are working with sets. Well, in writing we use sets too. We use sets of letters to spell words."

"See that dot? That is a period. I put a period (question mark, exclamation point) at the end of a sentence."

"When I write down what you say, I always start at the top of the printed page. I always start on the left side of the page. See how I write the words? I go left to right."

Developing Metalinguistic Awareness

In her paper, *Play with Language and Metalinguistic Awareness: One Dimension of Language Experience,* Courtney Cazden states:

If children construct their reality by playful manipulation of objects in their world, why should not their construction of their language involve playful manipulation of verbal forms, outside of use in meaningful communicative contexts? And if play is an essential part of the development process, then its presence or absence should make a difference. (Cazden, Courtney. *Play with Language and Metalinguistic Awareness: One Dimension of Language Experience.* Paper presented at The Second Lucy Sprague Memorial Conference, May 19, 1973.)

Children do like to play with language. Through playing with language they first become consciously aware of the fact that the sounds of language can be manipulated according to whim and pleasure. When children do play with language forms, it indicates a level of mastery beyond initial acquisition of those forms. Play with language begins at an early age and continues through adulthood.

Primary grade children are especially interested in riddles, jokes, rhymes, clapping games, jump rope chants, and counting-out games. All of these examples of language games share a common characteristic. They follow consistent, specific formulas. The words themselves may be nonsense words, but that is unimportant. What is important is that the formula must be preserved. In fact, in riddles, rhymes, chants, and verbal games of children's lore, the message is secondary to the form. The different versions of the counting-out games provide good examples of variations of words and standardization of form. There are, for example, international versions of "Eeny Meeny" and "One Potato Two Potato." These versions vary only in words but *never* in actual rhyming pattern or rhythm. These are the first lines of variations of "Eeny Meeny" found in various countries:

Eena, meena, micka, macka (Australia)
Eeny, meeny, mack-a, rack-a (England)
Ene mene mu (Germany)
Eeny, meeny, cho cha beeny (United States)

The basic requirements are that the lines rhyme and that the rhythm be consistent.

Whether it is a riddle or a jump rope chant, as the above examples illustrate, a formula is followed. Because of this emphasis on form rather than content, children's lore can be used to teach the symbolic, printed form of oral language. Knock Knock jokes can show the relationship between oral and written expression while also illustrating the purpose of standard usage and written forms.

Knock! Knock! (exclamation points)
Who's there? (question marks and contractions)
Boo.
Boo who?
Well, you don't have to cry about it!

Riddles, clapping games, and rhymes provide repetition that children themselves have preserved. Consequently, it is the kind of repetition that provides natural enjoyment for them.

A Step-by-Step Lesson

All children love riddles. Often they do not know the subtleties of the riddle, but they do know that riddles are supposed to be funny. Children learn the formulas that signal that they are going to hear a riddle or a joke. In fact, it is often these cues that trigger laughter. From the cues, they know that there is going to be a play with language.

What is black and white and red all over?

The cues may be, "What is . . .?" in combination with the raised vocal intonation that signals a question, or they may also include the fact that there are heaps of "What is black and white and red all over?" jokes.

Oh—the answer is, "a skunk with diaper rash!"

What does a duck eat?
A duck eats milk and quackers. (Angela Banks, age 5)

Sometimes the children are so familiar with the formula that they will deliberately switch answers.

Why did the chicken cross the street?
To keep his pants up.

Why does the fireman wear red suspenders?
To get to the other side. (Casey Standal, age 6)

Riddling can be enjoyed by adults and children alike, since they can compete as equals.

We want to give the right answer. We resist saying, "I don't know," even when it is hopeless. And often it is, especially when we are riddling with a first grader, who believes a riddle has only one right answer. Either you know it or you don't. (Knapp, M. and H. Knapp. *One Potato, Two Potato.* New York: W. W. Norton, 1976)

The following lesson expands metalinguistic awareness and reading readiness. Three to four days should be enough time to introduce, implement and complete the lesson.

Resource materials:

1. Sample riddles printed on chart paper or poster board.

2. Collections of riddles such as, *One Potato, Two Potato* (Knapp, M. and H. Knapp. New York: W. W. Norton, 1976) or *The Hodgepodge Book* (Emrich, D. New York: Four Winds Press, 1972.)

Introduction of the Lesson:

The teacher may begin by asking the class riddles similar to these:

What is yellow and goes click, click?
A ball point banana.

What happens when you cross a woodpecker with a chicken?
I don't know, but you have to saw the eggs open.

As you point to the words, read the riddles printed on the chart or poster paper. Point out the cuing words in riddles: *how, what, why.* Show the question mark that comes at the end of the first line of each riddle. You may show (or the children may discover) that the first line of a riddle asks a question. The second line gives the answer. Now, ask the children if they can ask the class some riddles. At the peak of their excitement with sharing riddles, show the children collections of children's riddles. Explain that some authors go all around the world listening to children and writing down their jokes, riddles, and jump rope chants. Tell the children that they can write their own riddles. After all, they listen to children all the time! ("You have so many good riddles, we must write our own book! Now I'd like you to think about a riddle.") As a volunteer tells a riddle, write it, verbatim.

As you take dictation, *say each word as you print it*. For example,

Why–couldn't–they–play–cards–on–Noah's–Ark?
Because–Noah–stood–on–the–deck. (Brian Baba, age 7)

Show the class that you always start on the left side and print to the right. Also demonstrate starting the sentence with a capital letter. Point out the purpose of question marks, exclamation marks, and periods.

After printing the riddle, read it back to the class pointing to each word as you read. Next, have the class read the riddle with you, pointing to each word as they read. This does *not* promote halting, word-by-word reading. Since the children draw upon existing oral language for their dictated materials, and since they say those words to you, oral language facility is transferred directly to this beginning reading. The purpose of pointing to the words is to insure correct sound/symbol identification. Children also practice left to right sequencing.

At the end of this group-writing period, you may ask them, "How can we find more riddles for our riddle books?" The children should discuss possible resources, such as other children, adults, parents, and books. The children should plan to find as many riddles as they can.

Each day of the lessons on riddles should begin with the whole group reading the riddles the teacher has transcribed on chart paper. Children enjoy the repetition, but more importantly, they are working with sound/symbol relationships, left-to-right sequencing, and, for some, developing a sight word vocabulary. Initially, these riddles would be written on the chalkboard at the end of the day. Then you would transfer the riddles to chart paper; new riddles would be added each day, with the teacher taking dictation.

Shy children who are learning English as a second language may be reluctant to ask other people for riddles. These children may work with buddies. Second language learners can collect riddles in their first language, as well as in English.

At the end of a few days, perhaps a week, the chart pages can be put into a big book. If you store this book in a corner of the room, children can thumb through it. You can extend the lesson by putting strips of paper and pencils with the book. As they look at the book, children can print words they recognize on strips of paper. Later, they can read these words to you.

Language Experience Lessons: Beginning Learners

Each of these suggested lessons employs the student objectives listed at the beginning of the chapter. However, beginning objectives for children emphasize the sound/symbol relationships and left-to-right sequencing. Consistently highlight selected objectives as you work with small groups, the entire class, or with individuals. Since each of these objectives does have a communicative purpose, stressing them in a lesson is natural, not contrived. As you take dictation from the class, you might say:

"I can print each word that you say. I start at the top left side of the paper. I print the words from left to right."

"I will print carefully. I start at the top of the space and pull straight down to the bottom of the space."

"This is a word. This is the first letter of the word. The first letter of the first word in a sentence starts with a capital letter. This is one way we know when a sentence starts. This is a period (or question mark). I put it at the end of the sentence. That is one way we know when a sentence ends and a new one begins."

"Words are sets of letters. We always try to spell words the way they are spelled in dictionaries. That way, everyone can read what we write."

"A sentence is a group of words. Watch while I write a sentence: 'Why did the elephant wear red tennis shoes?' The sentence starts with a capital W and ends with a question mark. The question mark tells the reader that this sentence asks a question. 'Because his blue tennis shoes were wet.' This answer starts with a capital B and ends with a period. The period tells us that the answer ends."

This procedure demonstrates visually and concretely the purpose of specific objectives. All objectives would not be introduced at the same time. Pace the demonstrations according to your children's needs and ability to assimilate new information.

LESSON 1: Add-On Chant

Children have fun with this chant (you should have it written on chart paper). The verses only go to ten, but the children usually insist upon adding more. It is particularly useful with second language learners because they can participate in a group experience without worrying about articulation or form. The class can compose its own rhyming words for the last line. However, the primary objective is to work with auditory memory, auditory discrimination, and sound symbol relationships.

When I Was One

When I was one (Hold up one finger)
I had some fun (Pantomime fun)

Chorus

Swimming over the sea (Pantomime swimming)
I jumped off a sailing ship (Jump)
And the sailors said to me (Point to self)
Swimming under, swimming over (Motion over and under)
Swimming to the White Cliffs of Dover
With a one, two, three (Clap once, twice, three times)

When I was two (Two fingers)
I tied my shoe (Pantomime tying shoe)

Chorus

When I was three (Three fingers)
I skinned my knee (Rub knee)

Chorus

When I was four (Four fingers)
I touched the floor (Touch floor)

Chorus

When I was five (Five fingers)
I danced some jive (Dance)

Chorus

When I was six (Six fingers)
I did some tricks (Children can decide a trick)

Chorus

When I was seven (Seven fingers)
I counted to eleven (Count to eleven)

Chorus

When I was eight (Eight fingers)
I stood quite straight (Stand straight)

Chorus

When I was nine (Nine fingers)
I felt just fine (Rub tummies)

Chorus

When I was ten (Ten fingers)
I fed the hen (Pantomime feeding chickens)

Chorus

Children may jump rope to chants, they may chant as they watch others jump rope, they may simply clap and chant, or they may chant and pantomime rope jumping.

> *Ladies and gentlemen, children too,*
> *This young lady's going to boogie for you,*
> *She's going to turn around,*
> *She's going to touch the ground,*
> *She's going to shimmy, shimmy, shimmy*
> *'Til her socks fall down.*
> *She never went to college,*
> *She never went to school,*
> *But when she came back, she was nobody's fool.*

The class should clap the rhythm of the chant repeatedly so that they can write additional verses that sustain the beat. Next, they should identify the rhyming pattern so that added verses will also follow this pattern. Dictation of these new verses should be a group lesson. That is, the children will work as a group in this lesson. You write the verse on chart paper, on the overhead projector, or on the chalkboard.[1]

All of the children may ask parents, primary caretakers, older children, brothers and sisters, or aunts and uncles if they know any jump rope chants. Individual children can learn these chants and teach them to the rest of the class. These new chants may then be recorded on chart paper. Each day, at the beginning of the lesson, read each chant. The teacher should point to the words as they are read.

The lesson may culminate by having the children break into groups of four or five. Each group chooses a favorite chant to illustrate. These illustrations could be murals of rope jumpers. The group chooses lines from their chant and those lines are printed on their drawing. The murals can be hung in the room or in the school hall. Since murals portray a story, they are particularly suited to the sequenced action of jump rope chants.

---

[1] Unless you print rapidly and well, it is better to use either the chalkboard or the overhead projector for taking dictation. You can then transfer the dictation to chart paper at a later time (after school, during lunch break, etc.). This insures that your printing is a good model for the class.

Children laugh uproariously at jokes—even when they are telling the same ones for the millionth time! These formulaic jokes provide a large resource for teaching material. Here are jokes told by youngsters ranging in age from four to eight.

Knock! Knock!
Who's there?
Duane.
Duane who?
Duane the bathtub, ma, I'm dwowning! (Connie, age 8)

What did one carrot say to the other?
Silly, carrots don't talk.(Doug, age 5)

What is black and white with a cherry on top?
A police car. (Eric, age 5)

What is orange, goes click-click, and is good for your eyes?
A ball point carrot. (Annie, age 7)

When is a dog not a dog?
When it is a puppy. (Sarah, age 6)

These jokes follow a familiar formula. They can be used to illustrate questions as well as the purpose of question marks and exclamation points. Since jokes depend upon word play, children can focus on word play through sound/symbol manipulation.

Knock! Knock!
Who's there?
Ether.
Ether who?
Ether Bunny!

You may use one of two approaches in teaching this lesson. One technique requires that the children collect one joke for each day of the lesson. The students ask people at home, friends, brothers, sisters, parents, primary caretakers, other teachers—anyone—to tell them a joke. These jokes are then tape recorded sometime during the day. Begin daily lessons by playing the tape recording of two or three of these jokes. As they play, write them on the chalkboard. You would focus attention on sentence form, sound/symbol representation, capitalization, all of the student learning objectives. The other technique is to record the jokes *as* they are told in class.

Evaluation: Beginning Stage

Each activity expands the child's metalinguistic awareness. The student learning objectives based on developing metalinguistic awareness are listed at the beginning of the chapter. Evaluation, then, entails assessing each child's demonstrated use of those learning objectives.

Children exhibit metalinguistic awareness by playing with language and by *interaction* with the teacher. The following outline for evaluation suggests techniques teachers may use that stimulate both play with language and interaction with the teacher.

Ha, Ha, This-a-Way

Ha, ha, this-a-way.
Ha, ha, this-a-way.
Ha, ha, this-a-way, then, oh, then.

When I was a little girl, little girl, little girl,
When I was a little girl, then, oh, then—

Work, work, this-a-way.
Work, work, that-a-way.
Can you work this-a-way with me, me, me?

Children should first learn the basic form of the chant. Individual children can take turns supplying verbs for the beginning of each verse. When the children are firm with the form of the chant, they are ready to begin their own verses. Children would choose their favorite action (such as running, singing, playing, eating) to use as the basis for their illustration and verse. Example:

Dance, dance, this-a-way.
Dance, dance, that-a-way.
Can you dance this-a-way with me, me, me?

Divide the class into small groups with the teacher working with one group at a time. Take dictation on the chalkboard, asking children:

1. Show me where to start printing.
2. When I print these words, where do they come from? How do I know what to print?
3. Why do I print carefully?
4. Why do I spell your words carefully?
5. Show me a sentence.

6. Show me a word.
7. Tell me when to use a question mark (or period).
8. Tell me when to use a capital letter.
9. Show me a question mark (or period).
10. Is reading like talking? (This should start an open-ended discussion with the child doing most of the talking.)

Another evaluation procedure uses an expanded version of this lesson. First the entire class dictates verses for the chant. The teacher asks the questions while taking dictation, calling on specific children or on volunteers. Next, the teacher writes phrases from the verses on sentence strips. Phrase and word strips are handed out to the children. Using a variety of clues (capital letters and punctuation marks as well as visual memory and visual discrimination), children match their words and phrases with the same words and phrases on the chart. Finally, the children with sentence and word strips must assemble them in correct order. Pupil performance may be recorded on a checklist or on anecdotal records.

Language Experience Lessons: Intermediate Learners

The ability to look at language deliberately and analytically has to be learned at the overt level. Metalinguistic awareness progresses from tacit to explicit understanding.

From about third grade on, many students become increasingly detached from and disinterested in classroom learning. Coincidentally, perhaps, at this point learning becomes more impersonal and textbook-oriented, and less tied with the students' out-of-school reality. By third grade, much of what is done in class seems to be a more complex repetition of what has been done before. As one eighteen-year-old said to me, "After first grade, it was downhill all the way." It may be that by increasing the distance between school reality and out-of-school reality, we are, at the same time, obscuring the purpose of institutionalized learning.

Raising the forms, content, and functions of language use to the level of conscious awareness—to the level of metalinguistic awareness—clearly establishes the purpose of learning and mastery of the following:

1. Decoding skills
2. Comprehension skills
3. Different forms of communication
4. Proofreading and editing skills
5. Legible cursive writing

6. Standard spelling
7. Complete sentences
8. Correct paraphrasing
9. Different forms of punctuation

Working with metalinguistic awareness detaches us from language so that we become masterful, powerful users of language. We cannot assume that students automatically understand the purpose of the lessons we teach. We can insure that understanding through direct teaching. Older students can regain their interest in language arts and reading by realizing that there is a reason for their continuing work with the form, content, function, and channels of language. That reason is to acquire power and control over basic communication skills.

Using comprehension skills in decoding, playing with words gives new life to using literal, inferential, and critical reading skills. At the literal level, students must simply recall the correct sequence of a joke (riddle, etc.). Catching the hidden meanings or tricks in a riddle stimulates the use of inferential reading. Critical reading skills are used in determining whether or not the class agrees that a particular piece of writing fits the guidelines for whatever writing they are doing.

As a teacher, you must consistently point out the *reason for* and the *purpose of* conventions in writing, as well as the functions these conventions serve for the reader. Lessons that are based upon play with language help to provide teachers with high interest materials for use in teaching both metalinguistic awareness and the practical use of "writing rules."

The learning objectives may be sequenced in the following manner:

Group A

The purpose of different forms of composition

The purpose of the mechanics of cursive

The purpose of standard spelling

The purpose of different forms of punctuation

Group B

The purpose of using complete sentences

The purpose and uses of comprehension skills

The purpose of word-recognition skills

Group C

The purpose of editing and proofreading

The first group of student learning objectives may be introduced with the first Language Experience lesson, the second group with later lessons, and the final objective used in a lesson evaluating the objectives in both groups A and B.

Oral tradition—the tradition of playing with language—allows children to be outrageous. Teachers need to clearly establish the rules before the lessons begin rather than after the fact. If you despise jokes about teachers, let the class know that you will not accept them. You can expect that some jokes or riddles will reflect racist and/or sexist attitudes. Oral traditions reflect the tacit or even explicit world views of their preservers, their perpetuators. These groups of people may be ethnic groups, age groups, occupational groups, and regional groups; and the potential for offense is quite real. Students should examine oral tradition as a reflection of values. Only by analyzing the implications of some jokes and riddles can students understand what kinds of damage or hurt they can do.

The following lesson uses play with words in a slightly different manner.

LESSON 1: You Tell Them . . .

Insults need not be damaging, but they do need to play with words; the more subtle the play, the better.

> *You tell them, pie face,*
> *You've got the crust.*

> *You tell them, coffee,*
> *You've got the grounds.*

> *You tell them, sand,*
> *You've got the grit.*

> *You tell them, peach,*
> *You've got the fuzz.*

> *You tell them, corn,*
> *You've got the ears.*

This play with words can reflect the current slang used by the class. For example, current slang at my son's college uses the word *booked*. *Booked* can mean either that someone has studied hard or that the student is leaving campus.

> *You tell them, pages,*
> *You've been booked.*

This activity creates funny visual images. Students can write and illustrate group or individual collections of these two-line jokes. Sheets of white butcher paper hung on walls and bulletin boards provide background for mounted illustrations and two-liners for class reading. Some of the butcher paper can be used for "You tell them, —" graffiti.

LESSON 2: Everyone's Oral Tradition

Children create and preserve their own oral tradition. Particular bits of the oral tradition emerge, vanish, and re-emerge years later. Have you heard this one?

> A teenage girl died—most mysteriously. At the funeral parlor, they unwound her long, heavily sprayed hair. As they uncoiled her hair, the undertakers were horrified to discover a dead black widow spider next to her scalp. The spider, trapped in the girl's elaborate hairdo, had stung the girl to death and then died.

Wide-eyed eighth grade students in my language arts class told me this story. It was also printed in the local newspaper. Years later I read a book on folklore that traced this same story back to the seventeenth century. Through the years, as hairstyles became complicated, the story emerged; as they became simpler, the story vanished.

Bringing the oral tradition of students into the classroom vividly illustrates the purposes of language use and language play. It hooks even the most disinterested student. It uses the language of students rather than the more distant language of textbooks.

This Language Experience activity focuses on bringing the children's oral tradition into the classroom. It can be introduced by reading from collections of folklore, such as:

Did You Feed My Cow? (Burroughs, M. T. Chicago: Follett, 1956)

Tomfoolery (Schwartz, A. New York: J. B. Lippincott Co., 1975)

Ballpoint Bananas and Other Jokes for Kids (Keller, C. New York: Prentice-Hall, 1973.)

Children's Games in Street and Playground (Opie I. and P. Opie. London: Oxford University Press, 1969)

The Hodgepodge Book (Emrich, D. New York: Four Winds Press, 1972)

One Potato, Two Potato (Knapp, M. and H. Knapp. New York: W. W. Norton, 1976.)

The class decides the form of lore they want to collect. It may be tall tales, jokes, riddles, jump rope chants, counting-out games—any or all of these. The lore may be collected from the community, from the school, from different groups within the school, or across the nation. Students draw an outline map of the target area (community, school, nation). Each day, they record a piece of lore and put it on the place of origin on the map.

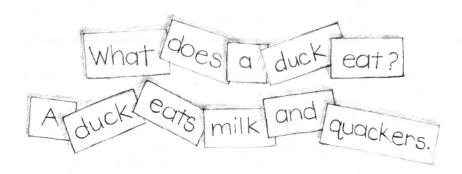

Riddle puzzles require manipulation of syntax. Riddles with their answers are written on sturdy paper and cut into word-by-word puzzle pieces. Students must reassemble the riddles and their answers.

In addition to emphasizing word order, this lesson also teaches the use of cues such as capitalization and punctuation. All of the students will need to use public writing in making the puzzles. In doing so, they will see the purpose for conventions in usage, spelling, and composition. The lesson crosses ability levels since it is as complex or as easy as the students make them.

Girls and boys who are learning English as a second language may use this game to help learn word order. Competition is not a part of the game, so there is no pressure to win. Students may easily work in pairs or teams.

The following lesson plan presents a slightly different and equally valuable approach to working with word play. The teacher who wrote it found it successful and fun!

IDIOMS AND WORDS WITH SEVERAL MEANINGS

The objectives are to develop

1. The understanding that words help form pictures in our minds.
2. The understanding that many words have more than one meaning.
3. The ability to recognize idioms and their meanings.

Materials needed

1. Chalkboard and chalk.
2. Paper and felt pens.
3. Butcher paper.
4. Bookbinding materials.

Implementation of the plan

1. Read *Come Back, Amelia Bedelia* to the class.
2. On the chalkboard list the words and phrases that got Amelia into trouble as the children mention them.
3. Ask the class why these words and phrases troubled Amelia. Lead them to an understanding that people understand one another because they have common experiences they label with common words and phrases. These become part of the language. Often the meaning is not in the words but in what they imply. Or a word may have a different meaning in a different setting.
4. On butcher paper list all the idioms and words with multiple meanings the students can think of and add the following examples:

rose	back	set	chest
light	slip	check	figure
trunk	plate	rules	club
run	racket	rock	star
bark	brave	trip	pitcher
hard	date	drive	fall
ball	scales	sink	

Encourage the students to keep adding to this list. The newspaper is a good resource.

5. Make a book to help Amelia understand our language. Fold pieces of paper in half. Have the student choose a word or phrase to illustrate and use in a sentence. For each idiom, have students draw a picture to illustrate its literal meaning and then write a paraphrase of the sentence to bring out the true meaning. For words with two meanings have the student write a sentence for each meaning and illustrate them. These might be bound in a book and put in the library to help ESL students.

6. Enjoy together some poetry using idioms and words with multiple meaning. Read "What Am I Up To?", from *The World of Language;* "Song of the Pop Bottles," and "Sit Up When you Sit Down," from *My Tangs Tungled and Other Ridiculous Situations.*

7. Make a bulletin board of examples of idioms clipped from the newspaper.

8. Rewrite the examples from the newspaper, paraphrasing the idiom by using its true meaning. Determine which is more interesting, the rewrite or the idiom. Lead the students to the realization that idioms add color to our language but make it difficult for ESL students.

9. The students might choose as individuals or as small groups to write a new Amelia Bedelia book with each individual or small group writing an episode. These could also be bound and put in the library.

10. The children might enjoy playing Charades with the idioms they have collected.

11. Enjoy reading *The King Who Rained.*

Bibliography

Allen, Roach Van and Claryce. *Language Experience Activities.* Boston: Houghton-Mifflin Company, 1976, pp. 108–109.

Brewton, Sara and John E., and G. Meredith Blackburn III. *My Tangs Tungled and Other Ridiculous Situations.* New York: Thomas Y. Crowell Company, 1973, pp. 5 and 39.

Forte, Imogene, Marjorie Frank, and Joy MacKenzie. *Kids' Stuff Reading and Language Experience Intermediate-Junior High.* Nashville: Incentive Publications, 1973, pp. 47 and 62.

Gwynne, Fred. *The King Who Rained.* New York: Windmill Books and E. P. Dutton, 1970.

Love, Katherine. *A Little Laughter.* New York: Thomas Y. Crowell Company, 1957, p. 49.

Parish, Peggy. *Come Back, Amelia Bedelia.* New York: Harper and Row, 1971.

The World of Language, Book 3. Chicago: Follett Educational Corporation, 1970, pp. 177–179 and T-130-131.

Prepared by Alice Newman

Joke Books—Illustrated Fun

Evaluation takes the form of an illustrated class joke book. Each student selects favorite jokes to include in the book. Since the book will be read by a general audience (other classrooms, parents, peers, people in the community) each student is responsible for considering the audience in choosing jokes.

This requires that the teacher read the jokes as they are handed in. Common errors should be identified. The teacher then writes a corrected version of the jokes on a ditto master. Copies of the corrected writing are handed back to the students along with their original copies. Students who make similar errors may work in small groups with the teacher, comparing their original drafts with the corrected copy. In this conferencing session, teacher and students discuss the practical application of student objectives. For example, what are the differences between the corrected and uncorrected copy? Do the corrections make a difference? At this time, the purpose for using legible cursive should also be discussed (did sloppy writing cause confusion or error in transcription?). Evaluation of student learning occurs in these small group conferences. Do the students know why the objectives are important? Do they know the purpose and function of these objectives?

While the teacher is working with small conferencing groups, the other students can illustrate pages of the joke book, compile the pages, make book covers, and assemble the books.

Language Experience Lessons: Children with Special Needs

Children's lore is something all children can share. For students who cannot run and jump, children's lore offers the fun of shared riddles and jokes. Children who need consistent repetition of language forms and children who need repeated work with speech sounds can work with songs, riddles, clapping games, and rhymes. Since repetition is what children themselves have preserved, repetition must provide natural enjoyment for them.

Clap, Clap, Clap Your Hands

Clap, clap, clap your hands,
Clap your hands together.
Clap, clap, clap your hands,
Clap your hands together.

Tap, tap, tap your fingers,
Tap your fingers together.
Tap, tap, tap your fingers,
Tap your fingers together.

You and the children may create as many verses and accompanying actions as you wish.

Juba

Juba this and Juba that,
Juba hugged a yellow cat.
Juba up and Juba down,
Juba clapping all around.

Let Everyone

Let everyone clap hands like me.
Let everyone clap hands like me.
Come on and join into the game.
You'll find that it's always the same.

Teachers and/or students change the directions (yawn, go up, go down, wink, stand up, sit down, etc.) as they wish.

LESSON 2: Categories Add-On

Another game children have fun with is Categories Add-On. It requires the first player to establish a category such as basketball stars. The first player names one basketball star, and the next player must repeat that name and add a new name. The third player repeats the first two names and adds a third. Each player must repeat every name given before, and must add one more name. This game teaches classification and adapts to a variety of categories (classroom, lunchroom, familial relationships, months of the year, days of the week. . .).

Language Experience Lessons: ESL Students

The oral tradition of childhood helps establish continuity between the child's home and school. Children learning English as a second language can dictate their favorite chants or riddles to be printed in their first language. Volunteers or other resource people such as aides can make a verbatim record of the dictated riddle or other piece of lore. This dictated material becomes reading material for the student.

Second language learners can teach their songs and chants to both monolingual and English speaking children, as well as monolingual non-English speaking children. This establishes valuable bonds between students while familiarizing ears to the sounds of other languages.

Teaching clapping games, jump rope chants, singing games, rhymes, and riddles in English helps students learn a new language in a happy, tension-free situation. It also provides a concrete context for learning new words and phrases in the second language. Because of the highly formulaic and repetitive nature of children's lore, it may help second language learners more than less-structured language experiences.

The beginning and intermediate lessons are all useful for second language learners. However, learning a different tonal system presents unique hurdles for most second language learners. Learning a new sound system often produces stress and anxiety, and playing with sound offers a positive alternative to more structured, tension-laden activities. The following helps students focus on American English sound/symbol relationships while playing with those sounds.

LESSON 1: C D B

You will need a copy of the book, *C D B* by William Steig (an inexpensive paperback book). *C D B* is based on decoding direct sound/symbol relationships. For example:

R U C-P? S, I M. I M 2!

Examples from the book can be drawn and printed on transparencies for use on an overhead projector. Students and teachers can take turns reading the C D Bs. As a class, they can make up their own C D Bs. They may then write and illustrate their own books. These books should be shared with monolingual, English speaking classmates.

LESSON 2: Chanting Games

Chinese, Japanese, Indo-Chinese, Cambodian, Mexican, Samoan are just a few of the cultures that play some form of chant games. These games establish a common sharing ground for all children. Students representing many different linguistic communities recognize the *ritual* of the game even if they do not recognize the words. The ritual bridges the gap between two languages.

"Rock, Paper, Scissors" (or "Rock, Paper, Fire") is one such game. Players simultaneously strike the palms of one hand with the fist of their other hand. As they do this, they chant, "One, two. . . ." On the third strike, the striking hand comes down either flat (paper), as a fist (rock), or with two fingers (scissors). Rock crushes scissors, paper covers rock, and scissors cut paper. Students can all play this game together. Once the pattern is firm, they may substitute different words and actions for rock, paper, and scissors. The new words may be written on cards. The teacher would model the nonverbal action for the word.

LESSON 3: Jump Rope Chants

Jump rope chants, with their strong rhythm and active participation, draw children into language experiences. Begin by having the children jump rope. Then add a chant either in the child's first language or in English. Some jump rope chants identify body parts. You may want to teach the names of these parts and their corresponding location before teaching the chant. This insures that students will associate the words with their concrete referents. Jump rope chants teach auditory discrimination, auditory memory, and auditory sequencing, as well as new words.

Chants written on large chart paper provide reading material for second language learners. Children read the chants as the teacher points to the words, modeling the reading in a fluid, rhythmic manner, just as it would be chanted in practice.

High-frequency phrases and words can be printed on cards. These cards can be given to children who may hold them up as they hear them read. Children may also match their cards with the words and phrases on the class chart.

Brinca, Brinca	*Jump, Jump*
Brinca, brinca	*Jump, jump*
una vez	*once*
Brinca, brinca	*Jump, jump*
otra vez	*again*

Spanish Dancer

Spanish dancer, turn around,
Spanish dancer, touch the ground,
Spanish dancer pat your knee,
Spanish dancer point at me.
Spanish dancer count to five,
Spanish dancer, dance some jive.

I love coffee, I love tea,
I love Lee to jump with me.
A, b, c, d, e, f, g, h, i, j, k, l, m, n, o, p,
q, r, s, t, u, v, w, x, y, z—out goes he!

Concluding Thoughts

Finally, children need to understand what *word* is, both the spoken word and the written representation. (Pflaum, Susanna. *The Development of Language and Reading in the Young Child*. Columbus, Ohio: Charles E. Merrill, 1974)

In teaching metalinguistic awareness, we use existing knowledge of aural language to teach the printed, symbolic forms of that expression. We literally show how playing with oral language can be recorded and become playing with visual or printed language. This is not merely esoteric, for children must learn that language, whether spoken or in print, can be manipulated. Without this knowledge, phonics, comprehension, and writing skills are never mastered in the truest sense of mastery. Knowledge creates personal power in the reception and expression of language. Furthermore, playing with language establishes shared bonds across cultures, languages and ethnic groups. It must be an integral part of reading and language arts.

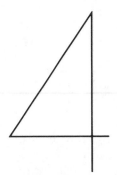

Transition: First Stories

Basic Skills: Reading

The student will:

Be encouraged to demonstrate appreciation for each others' stories.

Apply left-to-right sequencing.

Recognize upper and lower case letters of the alphabet.

Demonstrate knowledge that letters of the alphabet can be combined to represent spoken words; that these letters often consistently represent the same sounds.

Demonstrate knowledge that combinations of letters are often repeated because the same words are always spelled the same way.

Demonstrate knowledge that some words are used quite frequently and that these words become part of a sight word vocabulary.

Develop a sight word vocabulary.

Develop literal comprehension skills.

Develop inferential comprehension skills.

Develop critical reading skills.

Demonstrate knowledge that the purpose of reading is to communicate; to decode not just sounds but also to decode meaning.

Basic Skills: Language Arts

The student will:

Form upper and lower case letters legibly.

Dictate simple, 3–5 word sentences.

Capitalize the first word of a sentence.

Punctuate the end of a sentence using a period, question mark, or an exclamation point.

Demonstrate knowledge that the purpose of writing is to record a message either for oneself or for others; and that when the message is for others, certain conventions must be followed.

When you work with children, each developmental stage seems to be *the* most important stage. *Chapter 2* plays a pivotal role in reading and writing. *Chapter 3* establishes essential knowledge of the manipulable, flexible nature of language. *First Stories* establishes the base for developing as a meaningful process, word recognition skills, comprehension skills, and the mechanics of writing (punctuation and capitalization). Certainly this stage of learning about decoding and encoding can make the difference between becoming a strong, effective reader and writer and being a weak one.

With *First Stories*, children become individual authors. The activities in the preceding chapters have prepared the children for single authorship. As individual authors, students express themselves in unique, special ways. Differences in personalities and attitudes become evident through each child's response to the teacher's planned group experience. The child's response to the group experience reflects the child's individuality.

As the teacher takes dictation she or he learns about each child. The teacher hears the child's oral language production, and hears each child's own view of a particular experience. The class observes the teacher listening to and valuing the special nature of each child. This direct, visible honoring of children provides a model for the class, a model which they will begin to replicate in their treatment of each other. Typically children *do* respond differently. The following examples show just how different children can be.

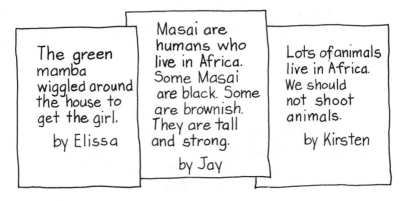

The green mamba wiggled around the house to get the girl.

by Elissa

Masai are humans who live in Africa. Some Masai are black. Some are brownish. They are tall and strong.

by Jay

Lots of animals live in Africa. We should not shoot animals.

by Kirsten

In our district, everyone had to follow the curriculum guides for a particular grade level. In social studies, the first grade teachers were required to teach units on Africa, Alaska, and the Pilgrims. Primary grade teachers can understand the foolishness of that requirement—first graders deal with the here and now, not the past and distant. My friends, Peggy and Louise, and I quickly realized that the only way to approach the unit on Africa would be to make the experiences as concrete as possible. We amassed as many films, study prints, records, and books as we could. Next, we asked resource people from Africa to talk about their lives in Africa. Over a period of two weeks all of our children shared these same experiences. Yet, as Elissa's, Jay's, and Kirsten's writing clearly show, common experiences stimulate individual responses.

Through reading their books to each other, individual children learn that different points of view exist and are valued. Teachers and children alike respect divergent thoughts, values, and abilities. This regard for single entities builds each child's own self esteem. It creates an environment of respect and appreciation.

Introducing Basic Skills

Students use a wide range of skills in each Language Experience lesson. The teacher gives one set of skills particular emphasis, realizing the other skills are also being used in a purposeful context.

In lessons on playing with words, group responses create group stories. Basic skills are introduced to the entire class at the same time. At this point, however, the pattern of teacher input/student output shifts from whole class dictation to small group and/or individual dictation. Small group dictation involves asking 2–5 children to meet at a writing area. Individual dictation means that the teacher moves around the classroom taking dictation from individual children.

Whether you work with small groups or with individuals, the procedures for introducing basic skills and for taking dictation remain the same. For example, if you want to teach the children to start reading and writing by looking at the top left-hand corner of the page, as well as teaching the left to right sequence in both reading and writing, your statements would remain essentially the same: "Find the left side of your paper. Now show the top of that side of your paper. Printing starts at the top left side of your paper." (Obviously, this must be modified to accommodate the story line that begins under an illustration.) "Watch while I print the words that you just said to me."

Basic Procedure

The Purpose of Illustrations

Typically, Language Experience stories include illustrations. Beginning writers, regardless of their age should use one illustration for each story page. Illustrations serve several functions for both the writer and for the teacher. For the writer, illustrations provide a direct, visual referent for the writing process. This visual referent can both stimulate descriptive language and focus the writer's attention on a specific topic or idea.

For the teacher, the illustration gives a shared referent for teacher/pupil conversation. This conversation provides the content for the dictated story. Children begin creating their stories by drawing, coloring, or painting the illustrations. This frees the teacher to take dictation. The children may go to the teacher in small groups, one group at a time; or, in the case of individual dictation, the teacher may move around the classroom, stopping at the desk of each child and taking dictation. In my experience, the latter procedure creates less total disturbance in the classroom because the teacher is the only moving body. If you plan to work with small groups, the entire class may start its illustrations before you begin to take dictation.

Illustrations do not need to be limited to drawing, coloring, or painting. They may be stitchery pictures, a collage, banners, carvings, or clay objects. A first grade teacher used the following plan with her children:

Objectives

1. Students will be able to verbalize about art work in small group situations.
2. Students will be able to share labels for artwork.
3. Students will form upper and lower case letters legibly.
4. Students will be able to dictate (or write) one or two simple, 3–5 word sentences.
5. Students should develop consideration and appreciation for other students' stories and artwork.

Materials Needed

1. Book: *Danny and the Dinosaur,* by Syd Hoff. (Kids do enjoy this book.)
2. Oil-based clay for each student.

3. Construction paper to cover desk tops.

4. Pictures of animals generally found as pets.

5. Books with illustrations of animals.

6. Lined paper for stories and labels of artwork.

Implementation (in story group seating)

1. Ask if any of the children have pets and elicit responses about the type, etc.

2. Read the story *Danny and the Dinosaur* to the group.

3. Ask children questions about how Danny felt, having such a strange pet, and how he must have felt when the dinosaur had to go back to the museum.

4. Ask children if they would like to have a dinosaur for a pet. What other kinds of strange pets would they like to have, if they could have any kind of animal in the world for a pet? Tell children they are going to make a clay pet that can be any kind of pet they want, and the class will have a pet parade along the windowsill. Each pet will have a sign that says what its name is and what it likes best. Send children back to work areas.

5. Hand out clay and desk covers to each child.

6. Demonstrate how to shape the clay by pulling out "pinches" into legs and necks, etc., or by adding "ropes" on a body piece. Caution against making legs too spindly. (If children seem unsure of how their animal should look, encourage them to look through animal books or study animal pictures displayed at some point throughout the room.)

7. As children finish their animals, ask them to bring their animal to a small group table, wash up, and then join you at the table. In small groups, they will dictate the name of their animal (with the help of the teacher if needed), and dictate a short sentence about what their animal likes best. They will also use this time for sharing their artwork and discussing the traits of each of their pets.

8. Place the pets along the windowsill as each group finishes its writing, with the writing behind each piece of artwork.

Evaluation of Lesson Objectives

1. Objectives 1, 2, and 5 can be evaluated by teacher observation while working with the students in small group situations.

2. Objectives 3 and 4 can be evaluated while working with the students in small groups and by looking at writing after work is completed and put out for display.

Prepared by Billie Mickelson

Taking Dictation

As you take dictation, you should stand *behind* the child, reaching around to place your hands in front of the child, just as if the child were actually doing the printing. *This avoids your blocking the child's vision as you print the dictated words.* It allows you to approximate the child's own hand position as if the child were doing the printing.[1]

At this stage in the development of the Language Experience Approach, teachers are still expected to take verbatim dictation. To change the language of the child devalues their beginning communication skills. Devaluing expressive powers reduces those powers and reduces both the child's belief that she can communicate, as well as the child's desire to communicate. Also, changing the syntax, usage, or form in print does not change that same syntax, usage, and form in the child's oral language. Consequently, when the child reads what she has dictated, the original, not the edited will be produced. A spoken, "I'm's" or "she's" changed to a printed, "I am" or "she is" will still be read as "I'm's" or "she's."

Teachers are often horrified at the thought of taking dictation for a whole classroom full of children. As mentioned earlier, one solution involves the entire class busily making individual illustrations for their stories. Since the drawing, coloring, or painting ought to be an independent activity, the teacher is able to move around the room taking dictation, or meeting with a small group for individual instruction and dictation.

Children who can write many or even a few words can help with dictation. As individual children acquire independent writing abilities, they may help their classmates. Older children from other rooms may also help with dictation. Many ethnic groups encourage older children to help with younger children. Perpetuating this ethnic value in the classroom helps to establish and preserve continuity between the home and the school. It also builds a sense of closeness, responsibility, and self-worth in the children.

Volunteers constitute another important resource for helping with dictation. Senior citizens can provide invaluable help, particularly for children who are accustomed to having older people share in their learning. Those children who rarely see older people need to experience a respecting and valuing of older, retired people. Also, the least we as teachers should do is to ask retired teachers if they would volunteer an hour a day to help in the classroom. Everyone benefits from this interaction.

---

[1] Avoid wearing any long, looped things around your neck. One day I bent over one of my first graders to take dictation, and my long chain dropped over his head. When I stood up, he came right along with me. Not recommended!

Small Group Dictation

Working with small groups requires a writing space where everyone can sit close enough to observe both the teacher and each other. It helps to have a small table where the group can sit together.

With the children seated around you, introduce the specific skill or skills being taught. The following example highlights the presentation of just one skill:

First, the children should be told that you are going to teach them something important about reading. They should all be watching you. "See, I can write down every word that Augustin says. He said the word, 'funny,' and now I print the word, 'funny.'"

However, with some children you need not limit the lesson to one skill. There are students who can process a larger information load. For example:

"You see, I start at the top left side of Masako's paper. I use letters to spell her words. Did you know that a word is spelled with the same letters every time you spell it? It is just like the way you spell your name the same way every time. Masako said, 'Kitties scratch.' Look, every time I print the word 'kitties' I will spell it k-i-t-t-i-e-s. 'Scratch' is always spelled with the letters s-c-r-a-t-c-h." (Show the consistency of spelling as you take dictation from the rest of the children.) "See, Annie said the word 'the' and I will spell it just the way I did for Eric when he said 'the.'"

After taking dictation from each person in the group, ask them to go back to their desks and finish their illustrations, trace over the letters in their stories, and practice reading their stories to each other.

The new group with which you are working may have finished a major portion of their illustrations. If they have, you can use the illustrations to introduce the concept of identifying the main idea of a story. For example:

> "Look at Tad's picture. What a marvelous lot of fish! Tad, tell us about your *picture*. . . . Oh, it is about a baby fish who got lost. Then your *story* will be about a baby fish who got lost." This comment consistently reinforces the relationship between the function of illustrations and the main idea of the stories the children write. Working with the main idea of their own stories prepares students for finding the main idea in both fiction and non-fiction.

Length of First Stories

Up to this point in explaining Language Experience, teachers are usually very interested. But now the question arises, "In dictation, how in the world do you keep children from rambling on and on and on?" From the beginning with Oral Language activities through Playing with Words, into and beyond First Stories, each child participates in *focused* speech. Focused speech means that the topic of conversation, discussion, or reporting is clearly identified and specifically addressed. Teaching children to focus their ideas and their language precludes unfocused ramblings. Furthermore, the illustration provides the main idea for the story and as such is a direct referent for both the person taking dictation and for the child who dictates. By referring to the picture, the person who takes dictation can provide a further guide in keeping the child on the topic. However, consider the child who can dictate a paragraph of focused language as one who can and should probably read that paragraph.

Putting Books Together

Most schools provide several different kinds of paper for young writers.

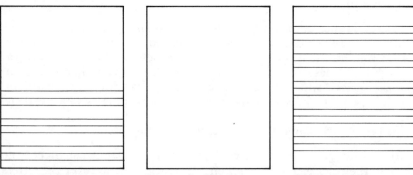

Figure A. Paper blank at top for illustrations and lined at bottom for stories

Figure B. Blank newsprint for illustrations

Figure C. Lined newsprint for stories

The paper in Figure A is convenient because the illustration and story can be put on the same page. The paper in Figures B and C can be combined in book form so that every other page is an illustration and every other page a story page. In either case, covers for books can be made using construction paper. Books can range in length (from two to even twenty-three pages). Most of the books average five story pages with five illustrations.

As you can see, the children write their titles on the covers of their books. They often include the name of the illustrator, too!

Before the children actually assemble their pages and covers in book form, you must carefully demonstrate the procedure you expect them to use. Show them how to put the pages in order, how to put the covers on the front and back of the books and, finally, how to either punch holes with the paper punch or to staple the left side of their books. If they are going to use paper punches, yarn should be threaded through the holes and tied. If the books are stapled, the staples must be placed as close to the left edge as possible so that the book will be easy to open and read.

This assembling of pages helps all children understand the organization of English language books. It is particularly helpful for children who are familiar with a different kind of book organization such as the back-to-front ordering one finds in Japanese publications.

Planning and Implementing First Stories

The basic procedure for teaching a Language Experience lesson is relatively standard, regardless of the stage of development within the Language Experience sequence or the stage of skill development of the student. You may follow this general outline:

1. Decide which skills you are either going to introduce, have the children practice, or that you are going to assess.
2. Decide how you are going to introduce and implement the lesson. (Will you use a children's book, a film, a guest speaker, a class discussion, a field trip, a record, etc.?)
3. Choose and collect the materials you need for the lesson.
4. Gather the class together. Regardless of the ages of the students in the group, it helps to have a central place where the class can gather together as a cohesive unit.
5. Introduce and implement the lesson. This follows a general pattern of: stimulus activity—discussion—production.
6. Have students express themselves, usually through some form of dictation or writing.
7. Have students share their work with each other, the teacher, other classes, parents, and, if possible, members of the community.

Language Experience Lessons: First Stories

The basic skills that should be taught through first stories are listed at the beginning of the chapter. You can introduce, practice, and assess the development of these skills through the lessons that follow or with ones that you plan yourself.

LESSON 1: This is My Family

I like to begin the school year by focusing on the child and home experiences. One way to do this is to have the children write *This is My Family* books. Introduce the lesson by showing pictures of your own family and by telling the class stories about your family. If you can, it would be even better to bring a member of your family to class. The two of you can talk about growing up together or any other shared experiences. On another day, you and the class can discuss the many different kinds of family groupings. Some family groups are mothers and children; some are grandparents, mothers, fathers, and children; some are fathers and children; some are aunts, uncles, and children. There are many different, many loving kinds of family groupings. On the third day, children can begin books about their families. A nice culmination for this activity is for children to invite a member of their families to class. On that day, children can read their books to the visitors.

LESSON 2: I See Me

I See Me books are stories about the children themselves. You will need to have mirrors for this lesson. I have used both small pocket mirrors and hand mirrors for the lesson. Begin by asking the children to look into the mirrors. Ask, "Who do you see?" Wait for responses. Then direct the children to look at their hair, their eyes, eyebrows, and ears—to observe their own faces. Next, have the children close their eyes and feel their faces, their noses, hair, lips, skin, etc. Explain that there are many ways of seeing ourselves. Encourage them to talk about how they see themselves with their eyes and fingers. How would they describe themselves? They will need to have plenty of time to look, feel, and talk. As you listen to them, jot down some of the things they are saying about themselves. On the next day, you can start the lesson by reading some of their comments: "Carlos said, 'I see my curly hair. I can feel it, too.' If Carlos writes a book about himself, what could he say?" When the children have warmed up and are eager to talk about themselves, hand out shape books for their stories. The cover and story pages may be cut out in the shape of a hand mirror. Have children draw their faces inside the frame of the "mirror" cover. Each writing period of each day, the children will write something more about themselves.

LESSON 3: *One Frog Too Many* (Mayer, M. and M. Mayer. New York: Dial Press, 1975)

One Frog Too Many provides a marvelous, nonverbal stimulus for an experience with language. This wordless picture book clearly and humorously communicates the frustration and jealousy one frog feels when it must share its space and friends with a new, cute frog. After seeing the book and discussing it, the children can use large sheets of newsprint to illustrate their favorite part of the story. Before giving the paper to the children, fold up the bottom edge of the paper so that it makes two or three folds. Leave this folded up until time for dictation. When you are ready to take dictation, unfold the bottom edge and write, using the lines made by the fold for lines and spaces.

LESSON 4: Camera

Most school districts have access to cameras. If yours has none, you will either need to use your own, borrow one, or buy one.[1] You and the children can take pictures of the school, the community—any interesting part of the environment. Each child later chooses a picture or pictures to write about. These individual pictures and story pages can be put together in a large class book. The book might have a single theme such as *Our School, Buildings Near Us, In the Country;* or it can reflect multiple themes such as *We Saw, I Like,* or *Many Things Around Us.*

LESSON 5: Shadow Tracing

Shadows fascinate children. In this activity, they can trace shadows cast on the walls, floor, or desks, or they can trace each other's shadows. Children record the location and time of shadow tracing. "I traced the shadow of a tree," or "This is the shadow of me. I stood by the window. It was 9:00 a.m." Place the shadow tracings around the room. Children can compare the size of different shadows with the size of the actual object or with the actual body size. They can compare the shapes of shadows as they change with the time of day. If your area has little sunshine, the same activities can be done using artificial lighting. (This activity may also be combined with science.)

LESSON 6: Books of Common Objects and Actions

Pictures of common objects and actions can be compiled as word dictionaries. Children cut out pictures of people, things, and actions. Pictures are glued on sturdy paper (such as tagboard), labelled, and compiled as individual word books. Magazines are good resources for these pictures. Sticker fun books can also be used. In selecting magazines for this activity, choose those that have many colorful pictures, and those that reflect different interests, (e.g., *Ranger Rick, Zoonooz, Sports Illustrated, Nuestro, Ebony, Ms., Good Housekeeping*). This particular lesson lends itself well to use in multilingual classrooms. Children can use labels in both their first and second languages.

---

[1] Simple cameras are a good investment for teachers. You can use them to stimulate learning, for keeping records and making slide shows. They are income-tax deductible if you use them as a teaching tool.

LESSON 7: Favorite Things

Favorite Things books are filled with pictures and stories about your class's favorite things. Initiate the lesson by simply sitting with the children and saying, "Do you know what I like? I like . . . ." (Some teachers might initiate the lesson by teaching the song, "My Favorite Things" from *The Sound of Music*.) The children should be encouraged to discuss some of their favorite things. You may point out that some of us share favorite things, but all of us have favorite things that only we like. The next step is to ask the children to draw pictures of their favorite things so that they can make books about the things they like. A twist to this lesson would be to write a sequel to the book, called *Things I Don't Like*.

LESSON 8: I Am a . . .

Depending upon the weather in your location, children can pretend that they are raindrops, snowflakes, puffy clouds, grains of sand, clouds of dust, etc. They should practice moving their bodies in imitation of one of (or a combination of) these natural phenomena. If you can, play music that would underscore appropriate slow, fast, gentle, or loud motion. Ask, as the children move, "How do raindrops move when there is a fierce, tossing storm? How do raindrops move when the rain mists and kisses our faces? How does rain move when it trickles down the window?" Rather than having the children draw pictures of rain or sand or snow, use things such as aluminum foil for raindrops, cotton for clouds, tissue paper for snowflakes, and actual sand and dust. Whichever element the children choose, the visual representation for it may be glued in patterns on the top part of construction paper. Stimulate the writing by saying, for example, "You are a piece of sand. You are lying on the searing hot ground. How do you feel? What do you see around you? What do you see above you?" The dictated story lines are written on the bottom of the construction paper. Or you can take dictation on a strip of lined paper and glue the paper to the bottom portion of the construction paper. Children can read their stories to the class, and the class can pantomime the stories as they are read.

LESSON 9: Maps of the School Grounds

Children need to learn that reading sometimes combines words with maps and charts. For this lesson, you need to bring in examples of simple maps. (Maps for children are published in social studies books as well as in *Junior Scholastic* and *Weekly Reader* publications). Introduce the lesson by asking the class why people need and use maps. Tell the children that they can make maps that will not only help them but will also help new students, new teachers, new aides, even a new principal. All people need to know how to get around on the school grounds. They need to know where to go to catch the bus, where cars are parked, where to find the playground, and how to find the entrances and exits to the school. When you are new to a school, you must learn all of these things. Have the children take pencils and paper with them as you take them out of the building to the school grounds. From this point on, you must determine how simple or how complex the maps will be. The children can simply draw the general shape of the school, draw the shape of the school grounds, mark and label the playground, the bus stop, and the entrance to their part of the building. Options are to mark designated parts of the playground (the part they play on, the path they follow from the playground to the classroom) and parts of the school ground (parking lots, any off-limits areas, their paths for coming to school and going home). When new children enter the school, these maps can be used to help orient them to the school, to the playground, and to classmates who enter the playground from the same direction as they do.

The following lesson illustrates how a teacher used Language Experience with a class of monolingual, English students and ESL students.

Objectives

The student will be able to

1. Demonstrate understanding of direction words and phrases, such as: right, left, straight ahead, forward, backward, up, down, stop.
2. Demonstrate ability to follow oral instructions.
3. Demonstrate ability to transfer a real, tangible setting to a visible form (a map).
4. Develop awareness that directions are to be observed in different settings, and also that they may have visual form.
5. Develop ability to direct others in small environment, e.g., home, school.
6. Develop awareness of why people need space orientation and the importance of understanding directions.

Materials needed

1. Boxes, pillows—any safe materials that can be used as obstacles in an obstacle course.
2. Blindfold.
3. Record—Palmer, Hap, *Learning Basic Skills Through Music, Vol II.* Educational Activities, Inc., 1969.
4. Posterboard.
5. Markers or paint.
6. Paper.
7. Crayons.

Implementation

1. Ask the class to copy your actions. Say directions aloud as you act them out. Example: "Put your right arm up; put your right arm down. Stand up; sit down. Lift your left leg up; put your left leg down." (Demonstrating understanding of direction words.)
2. Have children take turns being the "director" in the above action game. (Giving oral directions.)
3. Sing and teach the song, "Hokey-Pokey." (Understanding directions.)
4. Act out, with the class, the song, "Let's Dance" by Hap Palmer. (Understanding directions.)
5. Tell the class: "We are going to make a road in our room that is hard to walk through. It will have roadblocks on it, and you won't see them because you will have a blindfold on. You must listen to the person who is telling you where to go, because the road will be changed for every person." Move furniture aside and let the children set up an obstacle course. Have them show you the beginning, the end, and the roadblocks. Provide a blindfold. Children take turns being blindfolded, and once they complete the course, they become "directors." The road must change a bit for every person, or they will memorize it. (Emphasizes giving and understanding oral instructions.)
6. Tell the class that they are now going to draw the road and the roadblocks on paper. Now they will have their *own* map of the class road. They are to keep in mind the beginning, the end, and include all the roadblocks that are on the floor. (Shows transferring tangible setting to visual form.)
7. Show the class examples of signs on the street. Ask the children what each sign means. Ask if the class has seen a sign they do not understand. They can draw it on the board. Discuss what signs are for. Explain that they are directions we can see. Ask, "Are there

some signs in your country that are the same as some signs you see here? Which ones? (Shows understanding that signs have visual form.)

8. Have the class use posterboard and paint or markers to make their own signs. They may model them on street signs or make up their own. Encourage variety. (Helps understanding that signs have visual form.)

9. Tell the class, "We are going to use our signs to find places in school." The class makes a list of important places in school: the restroom, lunchroom, office, nurse's room, bilingual teacher's room, classroom, gym, playground, ESL room, etc. Children split into small groups and take turns explaining how to get from point A to point B in school, using their signs as props, but giving directions orally. (If you have an adult to help, let the children perform this activity actually moving around the school.)

10. Ask the class, "What happens when you don't know where you are going? What happens when you don't understand directions and you don't know where to go? (YOU GET LOST.) Have you ever been lost? Discuss being lost with the children. Let them share experiences after showing them the film, "Holding On." (Encyclopedia Britannica, 1969)

Additional activities

Have children create mazes to further illustrate obstacle course idea.

Make simple maps and write directions accompanying them, e.g., from home to bus stop.

Make treasure hunt games with road and roadblocks (three-dimensional roadblocks such as bridges, barns, houses).

Ask visually impaired resource person who is willing to come to school and talk about problems with space orientation when a person can't see and how blind people find solutions for these problems.

Prepared by Nancy Burke

LESSON 10:   I Like to Eat. . .

I Like to Eat . . . helps bring the child's home life into the classroom. Introduce this lesson by having finger foods for the children to eat. You could have chunks of fresh pineapple, sections of bananas, bite-sized pieces of flavored gelatin, pieces of cheese, wheat crackers—any variety of nutritious foods for the children to sample. As the children sample the food, inevitably one will say, "Oh, I don't like that!" or "What is that? It looks yucky!" Use these spontaneous comments to ask if they like tasting something they have never eaten before. Ask them if they have special foods that they do love to eat. Focus the discussion on the fact that we are reluctant to taste unfamiliar foods, but that what is unfamiliar to us may be quite familiar to someone else. In fact, it might be their favorite food. Tell the children that you want them to draw pictures of their favorite food. You also want them to write notes to the cook(s) in the family. These notes will ask the cook(s) at home to tell the child how to fix this particular, favorite food. The next day, after the notes have been taken home, and the recipes given, ask the children to write the recipe under their pictures. (Precise recipes are not important.) When they are finished, each child's contribution can be read to a buddy or to a small group. All of the pages can then be put into a book called, *We Like to Eat Different Things.*

Language Experience Lessons: Children with Special Needs

A teacher from Africa once told me that she found people in the United States obsessive and neurotic in their attitude toward learning to read. I explained that teachers and parents are deeply concerned that all children learn how to read. I pointed out that this concern is reflected in our providing special classes and special materials (sometimes with funds provided by the federal government) for students who have difficulty with learning how to read. The teacher burst into laughter and said, in effect: "That's a classic example of what I mean! If your children don't all measure up to some average, some testable standard, you plop them in special programs and inundate them with all sorts of aids. You tend to ignore the fact that the embarrassment of being in a remedial program, combined with often-dull, esoteric materials, may not help the poor child, but may actually add to what tests have identified as a 'reading problem.' It seems to me that you overwhelm children by expecting them to learn too many isolated skills. You take them farther and farther away from conceptualizing reading as an act of communication. Good heavens, I sometimes teach 75–100 children at one time—and my materials consist of a stick to write with and earth to write on. And all of my children learn how to read. I use their language and their experience. I don't need fancy materials."

For those of us who may feel that we need something more tangible than personal experience, research has shown that the Language Experience Approach is successful in developing the oral language abilities, reading abilities, and writing abilities of elementary school and secondary school students who have been tested and identified as having difficulties in learning how to read. (Hall, Mary Anne. *The Language Experience Approach for Teaching Reading.* Newark: IRA, 1978). I think that Language Experience succeeds because it relies more on the child's interests, experiences, and strengths than it does on pre-packaged answers that might not even fit the questions. For the slower reader, there is never the sweating humiliation of monotonous, word-by-word reading. Since the student has just told the teacher what to write, there is an immediate connection between the fluency of oral communication and reading.

The lesson plans suggested in this chapter can be used with all students, regardless of their ability levels. *This Is My Family* and *I See Me* are particularly good for children who have felt dislocated in school.

First stories for older students could center around more school-oriented topics. To expose their personal feelings at this point might be threatening. You can stimulate stories through lessons such as *Camera, Books of Common Objects and Common Actions,* and *Maps of the School Grounds.*

Other suggestions would be for the students to explore the school, learning the locations and names of the lunchroom, restrooms, principal's office, gym, entrances, exits, and the bus area. Students can learn to read the names of their teachers and the name of the school. Dictated stories could be an illustrated school directory.

You can also teach the students how to use such things as the telephone book to find emergency numbers. They can role play situations where they need to use the telephone book and the telephone to get help for emergencies such as fire, burglary, illness, or an accident.

If your town or city has a public transit system, the students can practice reading the bus schedule. Partners can make up different destinations, dictate them to you, and ask their classmates to find the bus or buses they would have to take to reach that destination. For example:

> "You are going to the show at the Roxy. You will leave from the Crossroads Shopping Center."

Again, lessons would emphasize that reading is an interesting, valuable form of communication. It has a purpose; it is a lifetime survival skill. All of these lessons work well with mainstreamed children. They are based on concrete experience and directly involve the child in sharing, experiencing, and creating.

Language Experience Lessons: ESL Students

All second language learners need to know that they are not alone in the world. Many people are, at one time or another, learners of a second language. To help develop this understanding, teachers should plan at least one lesson that demonstrates a valuing of a language other than American English.

LESSON 1: *Moja Means One* (Feeling, M. and T. Feeling. New York: Dial Press, 1971)

Moja Means One is a Swahili counting book. Each page presents a numeral, its name in Swahili, and a short piece about the cultures of East African people. You can read the book to the class and discuss different words that all mean the same number in American English. This is particularly interesting if your class is multilingual. Students can make a counting book (from 1–10) using their own first and second languages. The story line can tell something either about the child's country or the child's home. These books should be shared not only with the class, but also with other classes.

LESSON 2: My Shoes

My Shoes is both fun and informative. Basically, it uses shoes to stimulate the imagination of the children. You will need to collect 5–10 different pairs of shoes. The shoes should reflect various states of wear and tear, different sizes, and different functions. Before class starts, put the shoes on a table where all the children can see and touch them. Begin the lesson by asking the children to examine the shoes. After they have all had time to explore the shoes, discuss the people to whom the shoes might belong. Ask children to choose the shoes they think are the most interesting. Give them large sheets of paper so that they can draw pictures of the person they think owns the shoes. Underneath they can tell the places where they think those shoes have been.

LESSON 3:   *Pancakes for Breakfast* (DePaola, T. New York: Harcourt Brace Jovanovich, 1978)

Although teachers have called this book adorable, they have also called it ethnocentric. I think that it is less ethnocentric than it is location-specific. The story is about a little woman who wants pancakes for breakfast, but she is out of milk, eggs, butter, and maple syrup. She milks the cow, churns the butter, and gets fresh eggs from the henhouse. She gets fresh maple syrup from a neighbor who makes syrup. All of these activities make the book highly interesting to second-language learners. After sharing the book with the children, you can have the children write captions for each page. The book can be read with the new captions. Another activity would be for the children to draw pictures and write stories about the most important parts of the story. Another idea would be for them to draw pictures of and label the new words they learned from the story.

LESSON 4:   Magazine Articles

Older children want mature content in their reading, but they need easy language in first stories. You can read articles from teen magazines, from sports magazines, from any magazine popular with the students. Students must then retell the most interesting part of the article. Either tape record or quickly jot down what the student says. Finally, type or print their version of the article for them to use for reading.

LESSON 5:   Alphabet Books

Students of all ages can make alphabet books. Older students can use more sophisticated visual representations for the letters of the alphabet. They can make theme alphabet books (sports, music, art, etc.), or they can make alphabet books for young children. Alphabet books help children learn the letters that represent our spoken language, help expand vocabularies, and teach the system that is used in alphabetizing things such as telephone books and dictionaries. Younger children love alphabet books because they are colorful, and the text is not overwhelming. You can start this lesson by sharing many different alphabet books with the class. Some interesting ones are:

> *Jambo Means Hello.* (Feelings, M. and T. Feelings. New York: Dial, 1974)
>
> *Brian Wildsmith's ABC.* (Wildsmith, B. New York: Watts, 1963)
>
> *ABC of Things.* (Oxenbury, Helen. New York: Watts, 1971)
>
> *Project ABC.* (Rosario, I. New York: Holt, Rinehart and Winston, 1981)

The class can discuss the different ways in which authors write and illustrate alphabet books. Each student can then decide how to make and illustrate their own alphabet books. One possibility would be to use objects from the environment to represent the letters; another would be to use pictures illustrating a rhyming text.

Children can also form letters of the alphabet with their bodies. Take pictures of them, and use these pictures as illustrations for the alphabet book. Captions for the illustrations will be as complex or as simple as the age, interests, and language of the children.

LESSON 6: Squares, Circles, Rectangles, and Triangles

Working with shapes helps children practice visual discrimination and classification skills. Cut out large, colorful rectangles, circles, squares, and triangles. Mount them at the top of large sheets of butcher paper. With the students, look around the classroom to see how many objects represent those shapes. List the objects under the appropriate shapes. Walk around the school and playground looking for structures (signs, swings, fences, windows) and other objects (rocks, trees, clouds) that resemble rectangles, circles, squares, and triangles. The names of the structures and objects should be added to the lists. The class can cut or tear the outlined shapes of these structures and glue them to lined paper. They would then label the objects. An alternative is to give small groups of students long sheets of butcher paper. The students collect small objects and glue them to the paper according to their classification. They can also bring objects from home to glue to the paper. Make sure each object is labelled. Mount all finished projects on the wall of the room.

LESSON 7: What Is That?

This lesson makes repetitious use of the phrase, "What is that?" Tell the students that you want them to look in magazines and newspapers for pictures of unfamiliar things. These can be things found at school, in the community, at home, in the neighborhood, in grocery stores, department stores—any and every place where they might go. They will glue these pictures on lined or unlined paper. Underneath the pictures they write, "What is that?" By sharing the pictures with you, their buddies, and classmates, they can learn the names and functions of these unknown entities. The next step is to write, on the same page, "That is _____ ." Students can read their books to each other. These books should be left in the classroom as reference books.

Assessing Skill Proficiency

Assessing proficiency of the students can be either in small groups or on a one-to-one basis. I would suggest that you assess four or five skills at one time. In some instances, you can evaluate student performance through the daily dictation process. Pupil performance can be recorded by having a general skills list with the students' names on that list.

Student Names	Left-right sequence	Upper case	Lower case	Literal comprehension	Sight words			
Mario Gonzales	X	X	X	X	X			
Beth Maroney	X	X	X	X	X			
Andreas Snyder	X	X	X	X	X			
Christian Collum	X	X	X	X	X			

Skills are ← listed here

Performance ← Assessment is recorded here

Assessing the acquisition of skills should proceed by using the same questioning strategies outlined under assessment in Chapter 3 (page 59). And, as in that chapter, assessment must take place during a Language Experience lesson. Lessons such as any of those presented in this chapter provide the context for evaluation. Using skills in context reflects a more realistic determination of just how students will use those skills in the context of life outside of school.

The child's writing along with the record sheet shows the child's performance on those skills.

For children who do not demonstrate mastery of specific skills, you will need to plan further practice with those skills only. Two or more children who need additional practice with the same skill or set of skills can be put together for small group instruction.

If children have mastered the sound/symbol relationship and can accurately identify a word both visually and auditorily, they are ready to work at the next stage of Language Experience. Other skills that are not mastered can be practiced with any of the lessons presented at the next stage. Growth is not linear; one skill interacts and builds with others.

Concluding Thoughts

First stories are pivotal in the child's learning to read. For some children, this stage of development may cover a period of weeks; for others, it may take months. I have taught children who spent the better part of a year developing the skills necessary for independent reading and writing. I learned not to let this concern me. It is more important for the children to progress at their own speed—for them to feel and experience success every step of the way—for them to enjoy reading—than it is for them to be pushed into failure.

As the children dictate their stories, they see the direct relationship between the meaning and function of spoken language and the meaning and functions of language in print. They see that some words are used over and over again. These high-frequency words form the basis for sight word vocabularies.

Always, the goal of Language Experience is to teach skills within the context of purpose and use.

Pertinent Resources

Feelings, M. and T. Feelings. *Jambo Means Hello.* New York: Dial, 1974.

Hall, MaryAnne. *The Language Experience Approach for Teaching Reading.* Delaware: International Reading Association, 1978.

Oxenbury, H. *ABC of Things.* New York: Watts, 1971.

Rosario, I. *Project ABC.* New York: Holt, Rinehart and Winston, 1981.

Wildsmith, B. *Brian Wildsmith's ABC.* New York: Watts, 1963.

5

Independent Reading and Writing: Step A

Basic Skills: Beginning Learners

Reading

The student will:

1. Continue to expand sight word vocabulary.
2. Learn to use syntactic and semantic context clues.
3. Identify compound words.
4. Identify syllables.

Language Arts

The student will:

1. Write simple sentences.
2. Work with noun phrases.
3. Work with verb phrases.

Basic Skills: Intermediate Learners

Reading

The student will:

1. Apply the ability to use context clues in reading and writing.
2. Apply the ability to use structural analysis in reading.
3. Apply inferential and critical reading skills.

Language Arts

The student will:

1. Work with adjectives.
2. Work with adverbs.
3. Work with synonyms.
4. Work with pluralization of nouns and verbs.
5. Work with past tense.
6. Work with present tense verbs.
7. Expand vocabulary.

This is an exciting stage in Language Experience. Now young writers take their first steps into writing on their own, while older students move on to a more sophisticated phase of communication awareness and power.

Beginning learners shift from almost total reliance on the teacher to growing independence. They are encouraged to use sight word vocabularies as well as *their own knowledge of the sounds and meaning of language* to anticipate and predict word choice. Knowing which words can and do fit in communication means having a basic realization that reading involves the transmission and reception of messages. This realization was carefully nurtured and expanded through all of the preceding Language Experience lessons.

Teachers encourage beginning writers to use this knowledge by printing one or two words independently. The dictation process is essentially the same, but a subtle change occurs when teachers demonstrate to children that they can write some words on their own. This process involves drawing upon existing knowledge of sentence sense and upon growing sight word vocabularies. If the teacher knows that a child can read a particular word, a space is left for the child to write that word in. For example:

I went for a ride in _____ dad's new car.
We had _____ riding in _____ car.

There is a close match between high-frequency sight words and the words used in all writing. Sight words are often the "glue" for sentences. Repeated experiences with those words add them to both the reading and writing vocabulary.

Intermediate learners focus on the structure of written language. The ability to manipulate the structures of words and the structures of sentences increases both the precision and effectiveness of communication. Applying knowledge of oral language to language in print refines the students' word selection. Use of this language sense is an invaluable aid in using context clues for reading new and/or unfamiliar material often encountered in reading the content areas.

Word Recognition

Language Experience teaches basic skills within the context of purpose, application, and repeated use. Word recognition skills are utilitarian because they are learned through their actual function. Since they are taught with the students' own stories, there is no gap between the known and the unknown. The known is the child's own spoken language; the unknown would be how to decode that language in print.

Syntactic and semantic clues are used to teach more advanced learners to use context for decoding the meaning as well as the use of new words. This is an important skill because older students are expected to read increasingly difficult non-fiction in the content areas. Science and social studies use words that are not typically found in the listening and speaking vocabularies of students. The students must learn to use context clues as a major means to determine the meanings of these words.

Regardless of their ability levels, all students need to consciously study the predictable patterns of English. Early in their lives, language learners implement that predictability by using context clues for understanding new words that they hear used. For example, children are not expected to know the word *antique*, but if they hear it in context, they can gather the general meaning of the word:

That book is so old! It is old enough to be an antique.

Another example is the language learner's ability to use word order—syntax—as a clue for supplying unfamiliar words encountered in print:

I see six _____ playing ball.

Experience with seeing ball played, combined with experience in sentence structure and sentence sense, narrows our choices for the word that would fit the blank. All of our experiences combine to help us predict or anticipate the word that completes the meaning of the sentence.

And as the children develop further knowledge of the *sounds* of language and the symbols that represent those sounds, our anticipations and predictions attain even greater accuracy. When we can attach a symbol to the sound it represents, errors are further reduced.

I see six g_____ playing ball.

The process of anticipating and/or predicting takes less time to apply than it takes to describe its use. All of the pertinent information flashes through our minds; we supply the word and move on with our reading.

The preceding Language Experience lessons have prepared students for the use of context clues both in aural language and language in print. We first expanded their aural Language Experience and then increased their conscious awareness of language through lessons in playing with words. Next, we worked on establishing sound/symbol relationships. Now, in the developmental sequence, we are drawing upon all of this student knowledge to begin building word recognition skills.

Context Clues: Beginning Learners

We all use context clues in every day communication—when we talk with adults or children, when our children talk with each other or with us, and when we are immersed in using our language to anticipate and communicate. This facility with language comes into play when we supply words for unfinished sentences.

"You see, I thought he was going to. . ."
"Fall, I know. When I saw him swinging from the bars. . ."
"Yes, I almost fainted, too."

This kind of daily conversation resembles a game of "fill in the blanks" or verbal shorthand. Commercially produced games such as Password rely on this taken-for-granted sharing of syntactic and semantic knowledge as the basis for communication between partners.

Teachers can and should use this sense of language to help children become independent, self-sufficient readers. By deliberately teaching the practical use of context clues, we can teach most of the word recognition skills within the framework of the child's own printed stories. After all, children need to learn to apply these skills in context, and when reading independently.

Sight Words

Sight words are words we know instantly—words that we need not or should not need to stop to analyze. Unfortunately, most sight words are neither fun nor exciting to read and remember. I often had children who could read the word *hippopotomus* before they could read the word *here*. Words such as *here, there,* and *of* simply lack the intrinsic flash and dazzle possessed by words such as *spaceship, monster, lion*. In my opinion, lackluster words are most easily learned in the context of exciting stories. These are those sight words used repeatedly in the children's dictated stories.

This is me hugging my mom. (Mark, age 5)

Me and my sister hit each other. She's mean and I tell my mom on her. (Colleen, age 6)

Teachers can highlight sight words by planning lessons that give children reasons to use those words in their Language Experience stories. For example, Lesson 1 provides the written material for Lessons 2 and 3. The purpose of all lessons on sight word vocabulary is to show children:

How frequently they use high-utility words.

How these same words are used in stories written by other children.

How these same words are used in published books.

This not only provides practice with sight words, but also makes the transition from Language Experience stories to hardbound books quite natural. Authors share the language that they use to put ideas into print.

A very useful book of sight words (identified as most frequently mis-spelled) and activities is WORDROID, by Virginia and Tom Strelich (Reading, MA: Addison-Wesley, 1981). Not only is WORDROID useful at this stage (see following list of words), but it is also of benefit in later stages of the Language Experience Approach, when students are ready for proofreading.

be	any	she	zero	them
on	for	had	give	help
is	big	run	find	they
he	get	ran	gave	late
go	but	yet	from	much
do	got	why	girl	play
no	can	win	fast	left
if	his	he's	here	good
it	boy	I'd	have	make
of	him	and	like	must
so	cry	it's	deep	sick
to	her	I'll	kind	many
in	did	I've	keep	slow
me	hot	you	been	none
or	bad	way	four	some
up	hit	red	glad	open
by	one	won	last	gray
I'm	two	man	just	work
a	six	fun	know	hear
I	ten	ate	goes	made
am	yes	try	knew	blue
an	who	how	gone	pink
as	put	tan	five	then
at	now	was	cold	will
eat	old	long	home	best
lot	new	come	once	with
Mr.	say	came	said	than
Mrs.	our	does	into	were
not	saw	done	park	take
let	out	down	says	when
are	see	away	stop	very
far	off	back	nine	tell

well	took	seventy	aren't	love
want	look	eighty	you'll	laugh
what	don't	ninety	front	cried
upon	school	hundred	throw	easy
wait	street	after	close	father
walk	loud	before	little	channel
fall	orange	right	there	telephone
went	yellow	playground	never	desk
recess	green	below	large	room
isn't	white	above	always	lose
this	black	haven't	small	book
won't	brown	hadn't	often	money
over	purple	didn't	television	read
we'll	three	couldn't	catch	math
blew	first	wouldn't	day	spell
can't	second	shouldn't	night	write
he'll	thirteen	what's	happy	score
she's	seven	that's	which	paper
we're	eight	she'll	their	drink
soon	eleven	where's	mine	ride
flew	twelve	they're	yours	think
warm	twenty	wasn't	sister	crayon
lost	thirty	you're	brother	bathroom
tall	forty	here's	pencil	mother
name	fifty	there's	sad	
near	sixty	they'll	quiet	

LESSON 1

For this lesson you will need to collect tin cans, rubber bands, paper clips, popsicle sticks, beads, cardboard rolls (such as empty paper towel or toilet paper rolls), empty boxes, paper brads, and beads. You will need enough materials for small groups of children to assemble a toy *and* for individual children to assemble a toy.

Small groups of children can explore and experiment with the materials, trying to create a toy. You will need to supply some direction in problem solving by asking them to plan what the toy can do, how the parts will work, and how they will put the toy together. Allow 15–30 minutes for this part of the lesson. Let each group share their new toy with the rest of the class, demonstrating the ways in which they have planned for it to be used.

Finally, give individual children a set of materials. Each child is to create a new toy. Encourage children to help each other with individual problem solving. This promotes cooperation and sharing, and it helps the child who is reluctant to work alone. Once the new toy is created, children dictate a story explaining how it was made or how it will be used. Completed toys and stories should be put on display for discussion and enjoyment.

LESSON 2

Write ten to fifteen high-frequency sight words on either chart paper or on the chalkboard. Ask the children to look for these words in their own stories (stories that they wrote in the last lesson). The children should circle these words as they find and recognize them. When they have finished circling the words, have the children print their names next to the same words listed on the chart paper or on the board. You should then point out that different people use many of the same words when they write stories.

LESSON 3

Put an additional ten to fifteen sight words on the chart paper or chalkboard. Make mimeographed copies of children's stories. (Again, draw from Language Experience Lesson 1.) For example:

This is a zooming toy.
It zooms all over the
place.
     by Francisca

My toy is not for little
kids. It could break.
Play with it on the
floor.
     by Sandy

The wheels turn good.
     by Andy

Children should look for and circle all of the sight words used in each other's stories. Listen as the children read and identify the sight words used.

LESSON 4

Add ten to fifteen more words to the sight word list. Using this expanded list, small groups of children should look for all of the words in newspaper and magazine articles on hand at school. The words should either be copied down or circled as they are found. Volunteers can then read the words they discovered. As each word is read, all of the children who found that word should say so. The class can keep a tally of the number of times a single word is found. If you wish, this lesson may be combined with math by having the children record the frequency of word use by bar graphs.

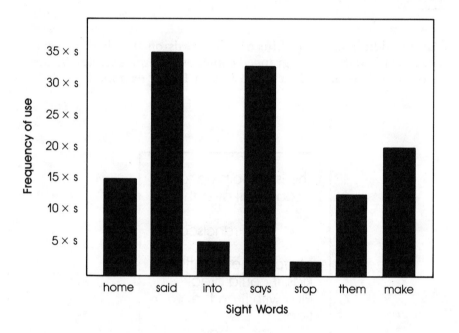

LESSON 5

Add ten to fifteen words to the growing list. Hand out basal readers or trade books. (The latter are books often thought of as library books.) Put the children into small groups. Have the children look for the sight words in these books. They should jot the words down as they find them. Every time a word is repeated, the children put a tally mark by the word. For example:

look III   is IIIIIIII   see IIIIII

The importance of this series of lessons lies in repeated experiences with the same words in a variety of contexts. Through this experience, children build a repertoire of sight words while developing the knowledge that many words appear over and over again. Through these lessons, children learn that in virtually any reading situation there will be words they know.

High-frequency word lists usually include about 200 words. They also cover a grade range of pre-primer to third grade words. Teachers can select words according to the reading abilities of either individuals or groups of students. In one classroom alone, words could be chosen from pre-primer, primer, first grade, second grade, and third grade. If you wish, the children can be grouped by word lists for the series of lessons.

Syntactic and Semantic Clues

These lessons focus on using a form of the cloze procedure to teach the use of syntactic and semantic clues. They also give children practice in working with noun and verb phrases. As the basic resources for their writing, students will use the books suggested in Chapter 4, the books of *Common Objects*, and the books of *Common Actions*.

LESSON 1

The first lesson should be a group lesson. Introducing a new lesson to the entire class draws the children together in a shared activity. It also provides the most efficient use of the teacher's time.

Choose one child's book of *Common Objects* and another's book of *Common Actions*. Choose three words from each book and print these words on the board. For example:

Common Objects	Common Actions
dogs	run
boys	stops
car	walk

Print these six individual words on six individual word cards.

Compose a story that would include those six words as subjects and verbs *but do not write those words in the story.* Where the nouns and verbs would go, put a blank line.

The _____ stops. When it _____ , boys _____ in front of it. _____ walk, but _____ run. I see the dogs _____ .

As you print the story on the board, explain each step.

"The first word of the story is *The.* I use a capital T because it is the first letter of the first word of the sentence. I will put a blank line where the next word goes because I want you to guess which word belongs there."

Read through the words you have printed on the chalkboard. Begin to read the story. Pause at the blank spaces and ask the children to decide which of the six words goes in the blank. If you wish, you may say, "We need a word that tells who (or what). We need a word that tells what someone or something did." As the word is supplied, give one of the children the card with that word printed on it. The child will then go to the board and print the word on the blank line.

Select two more children's books of *Common Objects* and *Common Actions* and repeat the procedure. I think you should probably stop here for the day. On the following day, repeat the procedure once. Then tell the children that they are going to make guessing-game stories for each other. Each child will select three words from his or her book of *Common Objects* and three words from the book of *Common Actions*, and print each word on a single card. The children then write little stories, leaving a blank space where the noun or verb should go. At the completion of the stories, children attach (paper clip) their word cards to their stories. Children then:

1. Select a partner.
2. Exchange stories.
3. Read the new stories and choose words from the word cards to print on the blank spaces.
4. Partners read the completed stories to each other.

The lesson should be repeated several times. Teachers can assess each student's development of syntactic and semantic understanding by reading the completed stories.

LESSON 2

Repeat the preceding lesson adding the initial consonant of the word both as an additional visual clue and as introductory experience with initial consonants. If the word should begin with a vowel, the entire word should be deleted. I believe that phonics lessons should begin with consonants because they are more consistent in their sound/symbol relationship than are most vowels. Children look for the word on the word card that begins with the same initial consonant as is indicated at the beginning of the blank. Semantic-knowledge checks insure that the chosen word makes sense in the context of the sentence.

My grandma s———— on a bee. My m-———— really l————.

One primary grade teacher introduced the use of context clues through the following Language Experience lesson:

DEVELOPING LISTENING SKILLS AND A "SOUND VOCABULARY"

Objectives

The student will develop:

1. Awareness of the variety and meaning of environmental sounds.
2. Auditory discrimination.
3. Vocabulary for describing sounds.
4. The ability to use context clues in reading.
5. Ability to participate in group discussion.
6. Ability to write descriptively about sounds.
7. Ability to use exclamation marks correctly.
8. An interest in sound sources and an ability to formulate questions about sound and hearing.

PART 1

Materials needed

Lined and plain paper for writing and illustrating; crayons, pencils, pens, etc., for illustrating; construction paper for book covers; book: *The Listening Walk.*

Step 1: Students assemble blank pages to become their *I Like to Listen* books. They may be made as shape books in the shape of ears if desired. Students draw cover designs appropriate to the topic.

Step 2: The teacher reads *The Listening Walk* to the class. As it is being read, the class talks about how many of the sounds the book describes that the students have heard before and those they have not heard. Students are asked to contribute other sounds they think of as the story is read.

Step 3: The class goes on a "listening walk." Students are asked to be very quiet and to pay attention to all the different sounds they hear.

Step 4: The class discusses all the different sounds they heard and the teacher lists them on the board.

Step 5: Students are asked to draw pictures of things they heard on their "listening walk" that made a noise.

Step 6: Students write sentences to tell about the sounds that are shown in their pictures. The teacher helps students to use exclamation points when writing about sharp or loud noises.

Step 7: Students pair up and read each other their stories.

PART 2

Materials needed

Listening books that students previously made; materials for illustrating; books: *All Sizes of Noises, Sound Words;* noise-making objects, such as a bell, an alarm clock, breakfast cereal in a box, cellophane.

Step 1: Teacher reads *All Sizes of Noises* and *Sound Words.* As the stories are being read, the class discusses and acts out what sound words stand for, such as *clumpety, crunch, gulp, click, screech, thud,* etc.

Step 2: After the stories are read, ask the students to think about all the different sound words that were in the stories and any others they can think of. Make a wall chart using all the responses.

Step 3: The class plays a listening game. The teacher has previously assembled a number of noise-making objects. Actions such as knocking on different objects, writing on the chalkboard, washing a mirror, stacking books are also used.

The game is played as follows: All the students are given an opportunity to listen to all of the sounds that will be used in the game. Then each student, one at a time, is blindfolded. The teacher makes one of the sounds while all the students listen. The blindfold is removed and the student tries to guess which object made the sound. Then the student selects a sound word or words to describe the student's "own word." The next child takes a turn and this continues until all have played. The word or words they select are printed (or students can print them) on cards for them to keep.

Step 4: Students draw pictures of their favorite noise-making objects and actions.

Step 5: Students write sentences to describe the noises and actions they illustrated.

Step 6: Students divide into small groups and read their stories to the group.

PART 3

Materials needed

A tape of environmental sounds; book: *Crash! Bang! Boom!*; magazines or old catalogs with pictures of household items; scissors; paste or glue.

Step 1: Play a tape of environmental sounds. After each sound is played, discuss the students' ideas of what the sound is. Then discuss the various meanings of different sounds—alarms, sirens, etc.

Step 2: Read and show the book *Crash! Bang! Boom!* to the class.

Step 3: Give the students a homework assignment to make lists of all the things in their homes that make sound.

Step 4: Discuss in class the household items that the students listed. Discuss items that were the same in many homes and those that were more unusual.

Step 5: Have students begin working on a group collage of household items that make sounds. Pictures are cut from magazines and pasted on a large sheet of butcher paper. Students decide as a group on a title for the collage. The students may write short captions on the finished collage using sound words for the pictured items. The completed collage is displayed in the classroom.

PART 4

Materials needed

Sentence completion worksheets, which are lists of incomplete sentences; individual *I Like to Listen* books.

Step 1: Give students lists of incomplete sentences:

The campfire _____ as it burned brightly.

I heard the _____ of the rocket as it blasted into space.

The baseball _____ when it broke the window.

The boat made a _____ sound as it moved through the water.

The coins _____ in pocket as I walked along.

When I got my hair cut, I heard the scissors going

_____ _____ .

Have the sentences completed individually; then have the class discuss and discover the variety of possible responses used by the students.

Step 2: Have the students continue to add to their *I Like to Listen* books by drawing pictures of favorite sounds and writing about those sounds.

Step 3: Have the students complete their books and share them in small groups or in pairs.

Additional activities:

Books on related topics such as books about the five senses, how we hear, or about the nature of sound can be provided for students. These could then become their reading books for the week, which would include individual reading practice, oral reading, and discussion with the teacher and with other students about their books. Other language experience lessons on these related topics could follow.

Some books on related topics are:

1. *My Five Senses* by Aliki (1962)
2. *Our Senses and How they Work* by Herbert S. Zim (1956)
3. *Your Ears* by Irving and Ruth Adler (1963)

Bibliography

All Sizes of Noises by Karla Kuskin; Harper and Row (1963)

Crash! Bang! Boom! by Peter Spier; Doubleday and Co. (1972)

The Listening Walk by Paul Showers; Thomas Y. Crowell Co. (1961)

Sound Words by Joan Hanson; Lerner Publications (1976)

Prepared by Charlotte Garinger

Compound Words

The introduction of compound words prepares children for dividing words into syllables. If children see that a word such as *mailbox* can become *mail . . . box*, and still retain its meaning, they will more readily understand that *happy* can become hap . . . py and still retain its meaning. Just as,

 t . . . an is tan
 p . . . an is pan
 sp . . . an is span
 pl . . . an is plan
 fl . . . an is flan

Compound words may be introduced either inductively or deductively. The next lesson uses deductive teaching because it more closely matches the learning styles of field-sensitive children. The latter learn better when instruction first presents the entire rule and/or procedure and then moves to an analysis of the parts. Many primary grade children are field-sensitive.

LESSON 1

You may begin by explaining that we sometimes make one word by putting two words together. Say the following words as you print them.

 rain + bow = rainbow
 air + plane = airplane
 space + ship = spaceship
 night + gown = nightgown

Ask the children to give their own examples of compound words. As they are given, print the words on the board. Ask the children if their ears can hear the two words in the compound word. As volunteers continue to give their examples of compound words, have them pause between the two words. For example:

 foot (pause) print

After the children have gone for the day, transcribe these compound words on chart paper.

LESSON 2

Review the compound words from Lesson 1. Ask the children if they found any additional examples of compound words. Add those words to your list. Have children select their favorite compound words. Ask them to add these words to each *Book of Common Objects*.

LESSON 3

Children are to choose 1–4 compound words from their books. On plain paper they illustrate each single word that composes the compound word. This is not as easy as it sounds, but it is fun and provides a visual image of the compound word. It also illustrates individual differences in responses to the same word. The word *downstream* will be illustrated according to each child's image for the word *down* and the image for the word *stream*. When the illustrations are complete, the children turn their papers over and, in small, light letters, print their compound words. Children then exchange papers and try to guess each other's compound words. At the end of the lesson, papers should be displayed around the classroom.

Syllables

Work with syllables actually began in Chapter 3, "Playing with Words: Metalinguistic Awareness." Children supplied words that fit the rhythm of the chants. Those same chants can now be used in lessons on syllables.

LESSON 1

"Juba" uses one- and two-syllable words.

> *Juba this and Juba that,*
> *Juba hugged a yellow cat.*
> *Juba up and Juba down,*
> *Juba clap . . . ping all around.*

By clapping the rhythm of each of the words in each line of "Juba," children practice auditory discrimination of syllables.

LESSON 2

Using "Juba," delete the second word in the last line. Children must supply one word for that blank, and that word must have two claps just like the word "clapping." You may also want to delete the second word and the fifth word in the third line, with the children supplying the new two clap words. Actually, you can delete almost any word in the chant; just make sure that the children first determine the number of claps the new word must have.

Pronounce a series of words. Have the children clap the parts of the words.

Momma	dragon	truck	donkey
baby	elephant	monster	helicopter
teacher	car	octopus	spider

Now print those words on the board. Ask the children to clap the words as you say them. As they are clapped, divide the words into syllables:

drag/on el/e/phant spi/der

Explain that you can make a mark between each clap. These marks (slashes) show how words have parts—almost the way compound words have parts. Even when you divide them into parts, they still are the same words. We learn to put words into parts so that when we read a new word, one we have never seen before, we can use those parts to help us say the word.

As you can see, the combination of this sequence of lessons prepares children for specific work with phonics lessons. Phonics lessons are presented in Chapter 6.

Context Clues: Intermediate Learners

In reading, the need to use context clues never stops. Context can be combined with known sound/symbol relationships to help students pronounce words. Often this pronunciation triggers the child's listening-meaning vocabulary, and the unknown becomes the known.

Context provides other clues for readers. Sometimes the word is not recognized even after it has been pronounced. In that event, the reader must draw upon additional information: context clues.

> The girl, Emelia, inherited millions of dollars from her mother, a successful business executive. Now, as a wealthy *heiress*, Emelia may invest her money and increase her inheritance.

Applying inferential comprehension skills, applying an understanding of communication and language, and of sentence structure, the student can formulate an approximate meaning of the word *heiress*.

LESSON 1: Vocabulary Expansion

List a series of nouns and verbs on the chalkboard. Or you can mimeograph the word list so that each student has a copy. The words you choose should be common vocabulary words. For example:

boy	run
girl	walk
dog	see
cat	like
teacher	eat

The students must use either a thesaurus or a dictionary to find synonyms for these words. Each student then writes a short paragraph using as many of the synonyms as possible. Volunteers share their stories by reading them to the class. Teachers must emphasize that there is usually more than one synonym for a word. Students should discuss whether or not different synonyms alter the meaning or flavor of the stories.

LESSON 2

Alphabet books can provide a format for fascinating and creative composition. They also require vocabulary expansion. For this lesson, I recommend books such as:

Hoise's Alphabet (Baskin, Tobias, and Baskin, Viking Press, 1972)

The Great Big Alphabet Picture Book with Lots of Words (Hefter and Miskoff, Grosset and Dunlap, 1972)

I Love my Anteater with an A (Ipcar, Knopf, 1964)

Each of these books is infinitely usable with older students. They all have quite sophisticated content and illustrations. *Hoise's Alphabet* uses language in an interesting manner: "The quintessential quail" is certainly a departure from the traditional, "Q is for queen."

Ipcar's book is my choice for stimulating language and for providing experience for this lesson. His book is fun!

I love my anteater with an A because he is affectionate.
I hate my anteater with an A because he is argumentative.
His name is Aristotle. He comes from Afghanistan.
He lives on artichokes and asparagus, he is an abstract artist.

(Ipcar, *I Love My Anteater with an A.* Knopf, 1964)

Ipcar uses this old word game for each letter of the alphabet. Students may create their own alphabet books using this approach, or by using the unique format of *Hoise's Alphabet* or the multiple-word listing of *The Great Big Alphabet Picture Book with Lots of Words.*

An alternative is to have students work in small groups. Each group creates a shared book based on either of these suggested approaches. In any case, they will all be expanding their vocabularies by learning new words and by searching for uniquely descriptive words. You should allow a minimum of one week for the introduction and completion of this lesson.

LESSON 3

The previous Language Experience lessons provided practice with nouns, verbs, adjectives, and adverbs. The lessons stimulated the substitution of common words with less run-of-the-mill words. The emphasis was on vitalizing language.

For this lesson, teachers duplicate a short paragraph from a basal reader. In reproducing the passage, delete every adjective and adverb. Give each student a copy of the paragraph. Either individually or in small groups, have students fill in those blanks with interesting, descriptive words.

Make an overhead transparency of the original paragraph. Project the passage for the class to read and compare with their own versions. Discussion should focus on the precision and interest added by the use of descriptive language. This lesson also requires the use of inferential and critical reading skills. Students must infer meaning from the context in order to supply relevant adjectives and adverbs. Critical reading skills are supplied when the students compare their descriptive language with the original language.

LESSON 4

Choose particularly fine examples of descriptive writing, passages that establish setting and characterization. The following books are useful resources.

Ellen Grae, Vera and Bill Cleaver (New York: Dutton, 1977)

Child of the Owl, Laurence Yep (New York: Harper and Row, 1977)

Zeely, Virginia Hamilton (New York: Macmillan, 1967)

Arilla Sundown, Virginia Hamilton (New York: Green Willow Books, 1976)

Black is Brown is Tan, Arnold Adoff (New York: Harper and Row, 1973)

Harriet the Spy, Louise Fitzhugh (New York: Harper and Row, 1964)

The Dream Watcher, Barbara Wersba (New York: Atheneum, 1968)

Reproduce these passages in two versions. With one version, have adjectives and adverbs deleted, and ask students to illustrate the passages. Hand out the second version with adverbs and adjectives intact. Students should read the complete passages and modify (add to) the illustrations accordingly. Closure would be a discussion about added precision through descriptive language.

LESSON 5

Repeat the first part of the preceding lesson using samples of expository writing rather than pieces of fiction. Students should compare the amount and quality of information contained in the two versions. They need to discuss the importance of descriptive language in presenting precise information. Are there words that are, while descriptive, less effective than other words? Are there adjectives and adverbs that bias rather than clarify images?

LESSON 6

Give each student two slips of paper. On one slip, they are to write a brief description of a setting; on the second they are to write a brief description of a character or characters. Collect all the descriptions of settings and put them in a container. Collect all slips describing characters and put them in another container. Pass the containers around, having each student draw one slip from each container. The students read their slips and write a one-page story using those settings and characterizations. Have the students put themselves in small groups of four or five, and share their stories. Group members should assess the effective use of language in each paper.

Affixes and Root Words

Students have worked with nouns, verbs, adjectives, and adverbs. These experiences develop a heightened awareness of words as a unit of communication. They have studied the ways in which single words can influence an entire phrase or sentence. They will now study the ways in which word endings can influence the meaning of a single word.

LESSON 1

Word endings such as -s, -es, -ed, and -ing function as inflectional clues of pluralization and verb tense. The deductive approach is used to present these word endings in combination with root words. The following are examples of root words and their pluralizations that you can use to present lessons on inflection.

1 box + es = boxes   1 girl + s = girls

When students see a root word with an -es or -s ending, the clue is obvious, there is more than one object or person involved. Plural inflections in nouns used as subjects also signal that a plural verb will follow. Explain that singular nouns require singular verbs and that, interestingly enough, while a plural noun uses an -s or -es, some singular verbs often use an -s or -es.

The girl runs.   I teach fourth grade.
The girls run.   Kim teaches third grade.

The class should be told that an -ed ending signals that what is being talked about has already happened, that it is an action of the past.

I walk slowly.   You walked fast yesterday.

Just as -s, -es, and -ed are clues, so are -ing suffixes; -ing signals that a continuing action is occurring.

Walking is fun.

I was washing the car during the fight.

He hates running because it is exhausting.

Have the class work in small groups listing examples of singular and plural noun and verb phrases. When these are completed, have them list examples of verbs with -ed and -ing inflections.

LESSON 2

In Byrd Baylor's book, *The Way to Start a Day* (New York: Charles Scribner, 1978), she presents a shared folk custom of singing a song (paeon) to each new day. This tying of yesterday with today and the future requires that students incorporate -ed and -ing suffixes in their writing. After reading the book to the class and discussing this pleasant affirming custom, students can, either as individuals or in small groups, write their own songs to the day. They can use the noun and verb phrases and the examples of -ed and -ing verbs compiled in Lesson 1 either as guidelines or as resources for this writing.

LESSON 3

When the songs to the day are completed (Lesson 2), students can rewrite their songs, deleting the root word for all plural nouns, plural verbs, -ed and -ing verbs. Their papers would look something like this:

We _____ed and _____ed to the sound of the _____s. And, if you listen to the _____s swirling through the air, you know that we are _____ing and _____ing today.

Students can exchange papers, writing in words that they feel best fit the context of the song. Complete songs should be illustrated. Collect all of the songs and their illustrations and put them together as a class book. The book will serve both as a source of beauty and as a resource for noun and verb endings.

Deliberate teaching of the graphic representation of word endings is particularly helpful for students who do not pronounce those inflections in their everyday speech. These students may not be aware that those endings actually exist. I was reared in the West and rarely heard -ing word endings. It was not until I encountered the visual use of -ing that I became consciously aware of its existence.

Additional lessons in the use of suffixes and prefixes can be presented through approaches similar to the preceding Lesson. The use of this form of the cloze teaches skills in context while visually emphasizing the positions of prefixes and suffixes in relationship to their root word.

LESSON 4

The following is a Language Experience lesson planned for a combined class of monolingual English students and ESL students. The teacher who wrote the lesson works with a variety of linguistic communities.

DEVELOPING DESCRIPTIVE ABILITY AND PRACTICING PRESENT TENSE THROUGH USE OF ANIMAL PICTURES, ETC.

This lesson is designed for the intermediate grades who have reached at least advanced beginner English level.

The objectives are to

1. Develop ability to name animals represented in picture material (ESL students).

2. Develop ability to focus on describing an animal as precisely as possible through texture, shape, size, color, number, and action (ESL and English speakers).
3. Develop simple problem solving skills (English speakers).
4. Practice use of present tense, including interrogative forms (ESL).
5. Develop written language skills, especially with present tense forms and about daily activities (English speakers and ESL).
6. Develop listening comprehension skills (ESL).
7. Develop oral language through imaginative response to written material (English speakers and ESL).
8. Broaden descriptive language skills through creative tactile (touching) activity.

Materials needed

1. Visual material of animals: prints, picture books, slides, magazines.
2. Plastic miniatures of animals (optional, but desirable).
3. Potter's clay or homemade playdough.
4. Half-ruled, half-blank paper.
5. Crayons.
6. Book: Keats, Ezra Jack. *Pet Show!* New York: Macmillan, 1972.

DEVELOPING DESCRIPTIVE ABILITY

Implementation

1. If possible, take a field trip to the zoo (Naming animals.)
2. Display as many animal pictures as you have. Use animal picture books, prints, slides, or magazines such as *Ranger Rick.* Pass around animal miniatures and let the children handle them. Ask questions: "What is it? Tell us about it. What does it look like?" (Naming, describing.)
3. As you hand out pieces of clay to the children, tell them you want them to make an animal—any animal—out of this clay. As they model the clay, talk with each child. Ask what animal this is and what it looks like. If a child hesitates, specific questions may help: "How many legs does it have? How big is it? What does it do?" (Describing—see objectives 2 and 8.)

4. Tell the class, "We are going to play a guessing game. Choose an animal and don't tell us what it is, but tell us as much as you can about this animal." If there are no volunteers, the teacher may elect to begin this game. If a student has difficulty giving a description, encourage the rest of the class to ask questions in order to elicit their clues. (Describing, problem solving, and use of present tense.)

5. Tell the children to pretend that they can have any pet in the world. Pretend that the pet is kept at home, and that it is acceptable to the child's family. Ask, "What animal do you choose?" Ask each child at least one additional question: "What does your animal look like? What do you feed it? Where does it sleep? Why did you choose your animal?"

   Avoid asking questions in the conditional because you want answers in the present tense if you can get them. (Problem solving, use of present tense.)

6. Have the children draw this chosen pet and write about what they do every day with this pet at home. (Develop written language skills.)

7. Read *Pet Show!* Ask, "What is a germ?" and any other comprehension questions you think they need. Have the children comment on the story. Ask, "What pet would you bring to a pet show? Pretend if you want to. What prize would your pet win?" It is difficult to avoid the use of the conditional in these questions. Go ahead and expose the students to its use. *Do not correct verb tense in the child's response.* (Listening comprehension, developing oral language through imaginative response.)

Additional activities

1. Have children bring their pets to school, or bring photos and talk about them.

2. Ask if people in their countries have different pets than we generally see in the United States.

3. Ask them if they *used to* have a pet.

4. Tell fables of varied origins. Discuss characteristics of animals in fables.

5. Adapt a fable to dramatic form and put on a play. Make costumes and masks.

6. Discuss animals as symbols; these symbols differ from country to country or culture to culture.

Remarks

Accept all forms used in response to questions in these activities. That is, leave the child's usage alone. There is another time and place for correction. Use of time-marker words to elicit a verb tense is as far as the teacher should go.

Scheduling the presentation of these activities is the decision of the teacher. Half-hour pull-out classes do not permit more than two activities to be presented at a time. Sometimes one activity adequately fills one-half hour.

Prepared by Nancy Burke

Lessons for Children with Special Needs

Reading requires work with symbols rather than pictorial or actual representation of concepts and experiences. Writing requires abstract thought. Children must plan, select words, and compose expressions internally. Because of this abstract nature of reading and writing, some children will do better with writing experiences if they can use phrase cards for composing. Teachers can print a set of noun phrases and a set of verb phrases. Small groups of children can work with the teacher, with buddies, with older children, or with aides in composing sentences using the phrase cards. High-frequency sight words could be used repeatedly on those cards so that the children will learn to recognize them in context. For example:

Noun Phrases	Verb Phrases
The motorcycle	come here now!
A rhinoceros	went far away
Mary and Diane	is little
Christian and the teacher	fell out of this car
Paulo and Dang	ran under the dinosaur

As you can see, this type of lesson also teaches children to use punctuation as a clue in establishing word order. More phrase cards can be added throughout the year. Cards of adjectives and adverbs should be included as the children's descriptive language grows.

The following lesson is a variation of the use of phrase cards.

Objectives

The student will:

1. Develop an interest in reading (especially the child who is reading at one or more levels below grade).
2. Extend reading skills.
3. Learn relationships between spoken words and words in print.
4. Develop clarity in speaking.
5. Learn to focus on a single topic of conversation.

Materials

1. pencil
2. 3 × 5 cards, lined for accurate printing
3. paper (half-lined for primary grade or lined paper and blank paper for intermediate grade)
4. crayons or marking pens
5. binder

Implementation

1. Explain to the child that one of the purposes of this lesson is to practice conversing on a specific subject. Discuss the child's feelings when she is talking to someone and that person is not paying attention. Discuss the skills necessary to insure that people listen (adhering to the subject, coming directly to the point, focusing).
2. Explain to the child that as she speaks, you are going to record (print) some of the main interest words that she uses and other commonly repeated (key) words.
3. Initiate a conversation on a subject of interest to the child (sports, family celebration, trips, camping, etc.). The teacher should have perceived areas of interest to the child during previous sessions.
4. Develop a key word list (including only one word on each card) as the child speaks about her subject of interest.
5. The teacher will develop a story, using the key word list and appropriate reading level vocabulary. Care should be exercised to incorporate, as closely as possible, the original thoughts and ideas conveyed by the child during her conversation. Print the story on paper, leaving space for several illustrations. (Adjust this according to grade levels; more illustrations are needed for primary grades.)

6. Prepare for the reading of the story by practicing or reviewing the key word list or individual cards.
7. Have the child read the story. Reinforce the fact that the child developed the story from her own language and experiences.
8. Let the child illustrate the story.
9. Have the child read the story again.

Evaluation

Evaluate the Language Experience lesson on the basis of how well the child reads the story and by her overt responses (i.e., enthusiasm, expanded effort, reluctance, etc.) to the lesson.

Prepared by Wendy Johnston

ESL Students

Limited English speakers often rely on prefabricated phrases. These are set phrases that can be used in a variety of situations. Since the use of these phrases is a shared characteristic of second language learners, teachers can develop their own set of prefabricated phrases to help children develop sight word vocabularies. Of equal importance, the following also teaches the word order of American English syntax.

Sentences such as the following can be put on cards.

I am _____ .

I see _____ .

The teacher says _____ .

You have _____ .

School is _____ .

Give me _____ .

If you either laminate the cards or cover them with shiny contact paper, children can complete the sentences by actually writing on the cards with crayons, grease pencils, or felt-tipped pens.

Next, print sets of noun cards, verb cards, adjective cards, and adverb cards. Students assemble the cards in sentences and, eventually, in little stories. If you make individual pocket charts (see page

185) for each student, the cards can be assembled on the chart for easy reading.

ESL students are interested in the idioms of American English. Valuable experience with context clues can be developed using this interest. Native American English speakers can write popular idioms on phrase cards. ESL students can work with buddies, using these idioms as the basis for composing short passages that use context to explain the phrase. For example:

	The car had new brakes.
stop on a dime.	They were so tight that the
	car could stop on a dime.

Second language learners and children who speak a dialect (not ignoring the fact that we all speak more or less identifiable dialects) may delete final endings of words. At this time, you can teach inflections and final consonant sounds as they are represented in print. For example, the child may say col' rather than cold. You can teach the child that while it is perfectly acceptable to *say* col', that word is spelled cold . The same approach can be used to emphasize noun and verb inflections such as the pluralizations -s and -es and the verb endings -ed, -ing, and -d. The child may say:

We was runnin' fas'.

As you take dictation, you say, "Right, now when we *print* the words in stories, there is a *g* at the end of the word *running* and a *t* at the end of the word *fast.*"
The student who says,

"I have two dog."

is shown in the dictation process,

I have two dogs.

The fact that the child does not orally produce the -s on the noun *dog* does not mean that he is thinking of one dog. Generally it does mean that the plural is known but is simply not being produced in English.

There *is* a thin line between demonstrating the graphic representation of what the child means—what the child is actually communicating—and appearing to correct the child's spoken language. *The intent here is to demonstrate the printed form of their spoken meaning, not to imply that their oral language is wrong.* This may never, in fact, affect their oral language. However, the purpose is to highlight those word endings and final sounds as they exist in print; this is quite different from attempting to change oral language production.

Assessment

The assessment of student progress should take place during the lessons presented in this chapter. If you are uncertain about specific, individual performance, meet with small groups of children to assess their mastery. For example, you can ask the students to read new stories that contain the sight words you feel they should have learned.

Identification of compound words and syllables can be assessed by reading those words to the children both in context and in isolation. If the children cannot identify compound words and two or three syllable words, they may need additional lessons. However, if these children read well, do not assume that they need to continue working with syllables and/or compound words. Some children operate at the level of insight or intuition, and it is self-defeating for them to plod through lessons that attempt to teach them something they already know but have difficulty verbalizing. Word recognition skills are aids for reading; they are taught to help children become independent, self-sufficient readers. Children who already have achieved that autonomy do not need to be confused by being put through unnecessary hoops.

Assessment for intermediate learners is built into each activity. It should rapidly become apparent whether or not students are mastering the skills. Students who have difficulty with adjectives and adverbs may not know nouns and verbs. Such students should be immediately grouped for instruction similar to that suggested for beginning learners.

Remember, Language Experience lessons, by their very nature, require the use of the skills you are teaching. If these skills cannot be used, they have not been learned. If this happens, you should plan additional lessons that require the continued application of those skills. You must also be certain that you have told the children why the skills are important and what their function is in communication.

Concluding Thoughts

In this chapter, we have prepared the children for the more abstract word recognition skills that will be taught in the next chapter. We have also worked with the crucial skills of using syntactic and semantic context clues in reading and writing. All of these skills combine to give students the power of autonomous communication.

Pertinent Resources

Adoff, A. *Black is Brown is Tan*. New York: Harper and Row, 1973.

Baskin, T., and Baskin. *Hoise's Alphabet*. New York: Viking Press, 1972.

Cleaver, V., and B. *Ellen Grae*. New York: Dutton, 1977.

Fitzhugh, L. *Harriet the Spy*. New York: Harper and Row, 1964.

Fujikawa, Gyo. *A to Z Picture Book*. New York: Grosset and Dunlap, 1974.

Hamilton, V. *Arilla Sundown*. New York: Greenwillow Books, 1976.

———. *Zeely*. New York: Macmillan, 1967.

Hefter and Miskoff. *The Great Big Alphabet Book with Lots of Words*. New York: Grosset and Dunlap, 1972.

Ipcar, D. *I Love my Anteater with an A*. New York: Alfred A. Knopf, 1964.

Oxenbury, Helen. *ABC of Things*. New York: Franklin Watts, Inc., 1971.

Yep, L. *Child of the Owl*. New York: Harper and Row, 1977.

Wersba, B. *The Dream Watcher*. New York: Atheneum, 1968.

Independent Reading and Writing: Step B

Basic Skills: Beginning Learners

Reading

The student will:

1. Continue using comprehension skills as the basis for reading.
2. Recognize, pronounce, and use, *in context*
   a. initial consonants,
   b. consonant clusters, and
   c. phonograms.
3. Apply consonant-vowel-consonant phonics generalizations in decoding and encoding words in context.
4. Apply consonant-vowel-consonant-vowel phonics generalizations in decoding and encoding words in context.
5. Make the transition from student-written Language Experience stories to hardbound books (basal or trade books).

Language Arts

The student will:

1. Be shown the different purposes, functions, and forms of writing.
2. Write friendly letters.
3. Write reports.
4. Write poetry.
5. Begin working with paragraphing.

Basic Skills: Intermediate Learners

Reading and Language Arts

The student will:

1. Learn some of the different purposes, functions, and forms of writing.
2. Write for different situations, different audiences, and different purposes, using different forms.
3. Apply their own knowledge, gained through writing, to reading.

Beginning Learners

Each chapter in this book emphasizes using language in the context of the actual communication. Children have learned to read because they want to share ideas and experiences, and have developed the writing skills in order to record them. Through this reading, students have acquired sight word vocabularies as well as beginning phonics skills. The goal has been to develop independent readers and writers. The ability to communicate with decreasing help from others is directly related to the ability to problem solve, hypothesize, test, and draw conclusions about language.

Language Experience integrates the need for skills with the immediate development and application of those skills. Because of its holistic nature, it is not always easy to isolate skills and indicate *when* to teach *what*. Although this chapter highlights specific skills, it should be kept in mind that *these are not the only skills being used*. In any Language Experience lesson, many skills come into play; and this context-bound nature of Language Experience is most important in the teaching of phonics; if phonics skills cannot be used in context, they are totally useless.

In Chapter 5, lessons focused on using context clues for identifying and/or recognizing visually unfamiliar words. Context was used as a strategy for predicting appropriate words. This chapter will present lessons that expand the accuracy of this prediction. In reading, we all use our abilities to anticipate and predict; we use several different but related strategies that help us. For example, it is doubtful that you will read every single word in this book. In reading anything, we usually skim along, skipping strange words. If necessary we may go back to the skipped word. If it has nothing familiar about it, we use context clues to try to get the meaning of the word (but not the pronunciation). Should context fail, we may look at parts of the word or sound it out, but we usually ignore it or look it up in a dictionary if no one is available to ask what it means.

When you consider it, it is amazing how small a role phonics plays in the decoding process. I view phonics as only one strategy for identifying and recognizing visually unfamiliar words. Naturally, this (as is any definite statement about reading) is a controversial position. The teacher must think about the utility of phonics, and apply common sense to these questions:

Why do you teach phonics?
What purpose does phonics serve?
What is the function of phonics?
Can you teach a standard pronunciation for all symbols?
How reliable are phonics generalizations?

When I was in Texas teaching at an ESL institute, phonics was one issue that concerned teachers of migrant children. The impossibility of teaching uniform sound/symbol correspondence became quite clear when I commented that the book *Jazz Chants for Children* was an excellent resource for ESL classes. When none of the teachers could figure out what I was saying, they asked me to write the name of the book on the board (something I had to do more than once). They had difficulty with the word *chants*. They thought I had said "chance." We shared many such experiences because my Pacific Northwest accent failed to jibe with their Northwestern Texas accents. The teachers could use context clues—they could piece together and predict what I said—but where context did not suffice, neither did my sound production.

How, then, will I suggest you teach the use of phonics? We now step into another controversy. I think that children apply their knowledge of sound/symbol relations primarily to help themselves become independent writers. The lessons will focus on this.

Look at the following student writing:

My favrut thing at Emrld Park was when I divd of the dive. And when Richard and I spide everybody els in our room.

Eric, age 7

For Eric, phonics is functional. A teacher looking at Eric's writing would know that he applies phonics; he uses sounds in combination with spelling patterns to write independently. Because of the close proximity between his spelling and standard spelling, he will be able to read words such as *favorite, Emerald, everybody, dived,* and *else* when he encounters them in print. Obviously, by using Language Experience in the class, Eric's teacher taught the practical application of word recognition skills; and if skills learning has any purpose at all, it must be practical application.

Introducing Word Recognition Strategies to the Class

We usually think of phonics when we see Word Recognition. This limits the scope and comprehensive nature of several strategies available for use. Word recognition strategies are, quite simply:

1. Using sight word vocabularies.
2. Using resource people to simply tell the word.
3. Using context clues.
4. Using sound/spelling patterns (phonics).
5. Using a combination of all strategies.

Each of these strategies is given within the framework of Practice Reading (presented later in this chapter). They will be taught as part of the actual reading process, as children can apply them directly to their reading. Even though these strategies are presented in a linear fashion, all children may not acquire them in identical order, nor will children develop at the same pace. Because you have been working with the children in taking dictation and listening to them read their stories to you and to each other, you know their personal abilities and approaches to learning. Through organizational necessity, what I am presenting must be taken as a step-by-step progression; you should shape it to fit your children. For example, some children will be able to use phonics skills almost immediately; others will need continuing experience with establishing sight word vocabularies; and others may need more practice with using context clues.

The introduction and practice of word recognition strategies is given as you would present it to the entire class. The same techniques would be used in small group instruction.

Strategies 1 and 2: Sight words—asking others for help

Children need to be told that word recognition skills are important because they free them to read with a minimum of assistance. Bring the class together as a group, asking them to bring reading books.

You can say something similar to "Remember, we found words we know in many different books. Look in your books, and find words that you can read without any help." Give ample time for the children to find the words. If some children cannot find any familiar words, suggest that they look in another book for familiar words. Then tell the children not to worry when they do not know a word— they can ask someone. Ask the children to identify resource people who can help with words. Children should be told that it is acceptable to go on with their reading if they must wait for help.

Strategy 3: Context Clues

The entire class has been immersed in Language Experience stories. They have literally seen their talk written down. They have watched as their talk was transformed into print and then became reading material: books. What a marvelous bridge to context clues! Tell the children to remember, as they read, that the author is talking to them, just as they talked in the stories they wrote. When they come to a word they do not know, they need to choose a word that would fit the story. Show the class an overhead transparency you have made of a page from a basal reader or from one of their trade books. Delete words so they can practice using context clues.

> *Mouse, mouse,*
> *Come out of your* _____ .
> *Come out of your house,*
> *Said the cat to the* _____ .
>
> (from *Come and Have Fun,*
> an Early I Can Read book.
> Edith Hurd, Harper and Row)

Tell the children to remember that the author wants the story to make sense, just as they wanted their stories to make sense. So, what words would make sense in the blanks? Would it make sense to say,

> *Mouse, mouse,*
> *Come out of your pickle?*

Using several passages from the children's books, practice choosing the missing words that fit the story. Also give examples of words that would *not* fit. By presenting obvious contrasts (non-examples), the importance of context is constantly being stressed.

Once the children have reviewed using context clues, show them how this will help them be independent readers. "Sometimes when I read, I see words I don't know; I can either skip over them, or I can choose a word that fits the story. When you read by yourselves, you can do the same thing."

Strategy 4: Sound/Spelling Patterns (Phonics)

When teachers and students talk about sound/symbol relationships, they are really talking about sound/spelling pattern relationships. Our words are patterned, just as sentences are patterned. Furthermore, when children start lessons on spelling, or proofread their writing for spelling, we have pre-established the concept of patterns for sounds. The concept of patterns for sound *is* the basis for phonics. For example:

"The letter *p* makes a 'p' sound. These words begin with *p* and make a 'p' sound: pat, pan, pick, pill." (deductive)

"Do these words sound alike: *sat, hat, cat, fat, rat, mat?* Right, they all end in -at. A-T says 'at.'[1]" (inductive)

Material is presented on teaching sound/spelling pattern relationships as specific lessons for use with the children. The progression of phonics skills presented is similar to that suggested by Susanna Whitney Pflaum in her book, *The Development of Language and Reading in the Young Child* (Merrill Publishing Company, 1974). Keep in mind that the purpose of developing strategies in the use of phonics is to help children reduce the alternatives for the unknown word. Lessons based on this progression include:

1. Initial consonants (b, t, p . . .).
2. Phonograms (word families).
3. Consonant clusters (br, str . . .).
4. Consonant/vowel/consonant spelling patterns (pig, hat . . .). cvc cvc
5. Consonant/vowel/consonant/vowel (e) patterns
   cvcv cvcv
   (rate, pine . . .).
6. Specific patterns (-ight, -oa, -ai, -ould, -aught)

LESSON 1: Initial Consonants

The children have had experience with initial consonants in their sight word vocabularies (Chapter 5). This lesson moves into more direct teaching of consonants. The letters are grouped so that three or four letters can be introduced each week. This is only a general suggestion to modify according to the needs and abilities of your children.

Suggested grouping of single consonants:

Group 1	Group 2	Group 3	Group 4	Group 5	Group 6
d,s,t,m	n,b,l,c/k	f,g,r	j,v,w,h	x,z,y,qu	sh,ch,th,ph

---

[1] Although authorities in reading warn against telling children that letters "say" sounds (and of course they don't), I've never been able to find a workable substitution.

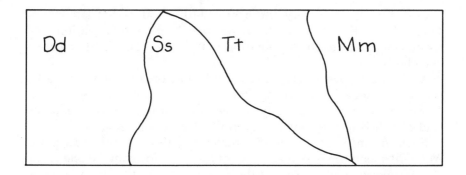

You will need a large sheet of butcher paper for each group of consonants (six large sheets). Each sheet should be divided into three or four sections, one section for each consonant. You will also need blank word cards, felt tip pens, pins, tacks, or tape. The consonants might be introduced by saying, "We have talked about the first letter and the first sound of words. If we know the first sound of a word, it helps us figure out what that word might be. You have seen me write letters when you tell me your stories. You have learned about the sounds of words. Now we are going to learn more about sounds so that when you see a word you do not know, you can look at the first letter of the word. You can think of the sound that letter makes. Think of a word that fits the story and begins with that sound. Learning about sounds and the letters that spell those sounds helps us to read and write without help from other people."

"Look at the paper I have put on the wall. Today we will learn about letters that go with the sounds we use in talking. The first letters and sounds we will talk about are d,t,s,m." With as little exaggeration as possible, point to the letters and pronounce the single sound they represent. Highlight the fact that the sound is the same for both upper and lower case letters.

"Does anyone have a name that starts with one of those letters? Right, Marcia starts with an M and Tony starts with a T. Print your name on this card and put it on the chart. Put it by the first letter in your name." Next, the class can say the sound, "M" in Marcia and "T" in Tony. Individual children should now volunteer words that begin with the consonants being taught. As a child says the word, print it on the card, and give it to the child to put by its matching consonant on the chart. Stop before the children run out of words. Review the letters, the sounds they represent, and the words that have been categorized with those letters.

Explain that when the children practice their reading, you want them to figure out new words for themselves. For example, they should look at the first letter of a word they do not know and think of a word that fits the story and begins with a sound that letter says. Certainly, initial consonants alone give limited information, but using context clues in combination with initial consonants narrows the choice.

As the week goes on, students should add words to the sound/letter chart that they learn during Practice Reading or during writing. Words can be printed directly on the paper, printed on slips of paper and attached to the chart, or even illustrated and mounted.

Each group of consonants is introduced through this procedure. You will spend the first three days of the week focusing on one group of consonants, and every day the children apply that knowledge to both their reading and their writing. On the last two days of the week, the class can review all of the consonant sounds presented, read all of the words that are on the chart, and discuss how learning initial consonants has helped them work by themselves.

Alternative Lessons

Children can make shape books for each consonant, writing in them words beginning with that initial consonant. Children can also make word books with two pages for each group of consonants, printing and illustrating words that begin with the specific initial consonant. Whichever approach you use, save the books or sheets of words so that children can use them as resources in reading and writing.

LESSON 2: Phonograms (Word Families)

Following are examples of phonograms:

at   an   en   et   un   in   on   it   ad   op   ap

The purpose of teaching phonograms covers more than having children make new, little words by substituting initial consonants. Ultimately, knowledge of phonograms will help children with spelling/sound patterns in multi-syllable words. Learning that some vowel/consonant patterns occur more frequently than others helps them to identify a new word. Seeing a word for the first time, they can combine strategies to decide:

context + initial consonant + phonogram = predicted word

As with anything, introduce phonograms by telling the children why and how recognizing phonograms will help them read and write with greater independence. Show the children a specific phonogram:

at

Demonstrate initial consonant substitution:

f . . . at = fat
s . . . at = sat
r . . . at = rat

Two or more phonograms can be introduced each day, but this introduction should be applied directly to reading and writing. Children must be encouraged to use the phonograms they have learned. If children ask you to spell or read a word that contains a known phonogram, tell them to spell or read the word by themselves.

One way to insure application is to have the children write a book of rhymes using phonograms. Another idea is to have the children write and read chants based on phonograms as the pattern for the rhythm and the rhyme.

> *I have fun*
> *Sitting in the sun*
> *Munching on a bun*

LESSON 3: Consonant Clusters

Consonant clusters such as:

bl fl dr str pl sw cr br sm r fr gr sn scr gl
spl dr

can be introduced and taught in a manner similar to that used in the lesson on initial consonants, or they can be used as an extension of the suggested lessons for phonograms. That is, rather than limiting the rhymes or chants to the patterns of phonograms and initial consonant substitution, the children could also work with initial consonant clusters and phonograms. Again, keep in mind that you expect children who have learned these spelling patterns to apply them in their independent reading and writing, and you must guide them to do so.

LESSON 4: Consonant/Vowel/Consonant Patterns

Learning to identify cvc patterns aids children in identifying and recognizing visually unfamiliar words. Since the phonograms in lesson two are based on consonant/vowel/consonant patterns (*bat*, *hid*), you can use the children's writing to teach the cvc phonics generalization. Remind the children that they have already worked with initial consonants, consonant clusters, and with phonograms. Now you are going to show them one more way to figure out how to write and read words. Write a series of words on the board (e.g., *set, rat, bit, top, fun*). Focus attention on the vowel in each word. Tell the class that a, e, i, o, u are called vowels. If you did not teach the word *consonant* in the lessons on initial consonants and consonant clusters, it is time to tell the children that the letters that are not vowels are called consonants. Demonstrate the cvc pattern. Have the children look at their books of rhymes (or chants) and ask them to write their rhyming words on a piece of paper. Children can exchange papers with each other and read these word lists. Tell the children that when they see a cvc spelling pattern, e will usually sound like the e in *set, bet*, etc.; a will usually sound like the a in *rat, ran*, etc.; i will usually sound like the i in *bit, sit*, etc.; u will usually sound like the u in *sun, but*, etc.; and o will usually sound like the o in *hot, top*, etc.

LESSON 5: Consonant/Vowel/Consonant/Vowel

Explain to the children that they are going to learn still another way to help them read all by themselves. They have learned about vowel sounds in cvc patterns, now they are going to learn about vowel sounds in cvcv patterns. They will see how change in patterns changes even the meaning of words. Copy several of the children's rhymes on the board:

I see a cat

Lying on a hat

Illustrate the way the sound and meaning of a word can be changed by adding a vowel (specifically, e) to the end of a phonogram.

I see a cate

Lying on a hate

Beginning Independent Reading: Transition to Books for Individualized Reading

Someone once told me that she believed that all of the child's reading material should be Language Experience stories. How limiting! That kind of denial of access to children's books is astounding. Children should add to their reading repertoire as soon as they have developed a beginning sight word vocabulary as well as other beginning word recognition skills. The reason for delaying children's using commercially produced books is that they first need to experience immediate recognition of words and know how to use context clues. Certainly this does not imply that books are kept from children. To the contrary, there should be books in the room. Children need to browse through the library and choose books; paperback books should be ordered for the class; magazines and other interesting, eye-catching publications need to be available for children to pick up and enjoy. A crucial reason for access to books is that too many children are fearful of failure in learning to read. Informal experiences with books help reduce this fear.

My son, Eric, cried and cried on his sixth birthday. We could not figure out what was wrong. Finally, at bedtime he sobbed, "Oh no, momma, now I have to read. Everybody reads when they are six." What a jolt for a first grade teacher to hear this from her own son! But Eric's fears are expressed over and over again by other first graders. Some children start school saying, "Will I flunk if I can't read?" "My mom says no boys in our family read good." "Do I have to learn what those little black bugs say? You know, those little black bugs that crawl across the page." How many times have you heard people say, "Oh, you are going to first grade—now you'll learn to read," or "You're in second grade? How do you like reading?"

In my opinion, reading must be demystified. We must establish a secure bond between children, their language, their experiences, and learning to read and write. By recognizing children as authors, we do just that. We demonstrate daily that reading is an extension of language. We demystify print because the children see reading as a personal experience, as a part of themselves.

Introducing Practice Reading

Actually not all teachers will want to introduce books formally. With books already in the classroom, individual children will naturally gravitate to these books and read them. However, you may wish to stimulate the children's increased interest in books through a whole-class presentation. You might say, "All of you are authors. You have written books to read yourselves and for other students to read. Many other people write books, too. Every day I read to you. I read books written by people who are not in our class. Now you should start reading them, too. See this book?" [Hold up an easy-to-read book.] I'm going to show you how easy it is to read." Read the book to the children, pointing out the words they already know. Next, have the children browse through the books in the room. Children should choose books they would like to read. If you are using basal readers, show the children that these books contain several short stories. Demonstrate the use of titles as a clue for the topic of a new story. You can draw parallels between collections of class stories in a single class book and the collection of short stories in a basal reader. The remainder of time should be devoted to each child's personal book selection.

Practice Reading

Learning to read requires experience with reading itself. My first graders chose the words *Practice Reading* to describe that experience. Every day, each child practiced reading for fifteen minutes. During this time, children read books they had selected.

Self-selected books often present words that children do not immediately recognize. Since the goal of any reading program should be to develop independent readers, it is within this context of individual, personal Practice Reading that teachers expand the child's learning and use of word recognition skills. First, you must clearly state the purpose of Practice Reading, explaining how it will help them to become independent readers. The children also must understand that the books they use in Practice Reading will be the same books they will read to you during individual, personal conferences.

Conferencing

There are other people to whom the child can read (buddies, aides, parents, volunteers), but every child must have conferencing—an individual, personal reading time with the teacher. To allow time for individual children, the rest of the class must be channeled into independent learning activities. (Chapter 8, *Organizing*, provides ideas for those independent activities.) Conferencing does work. Other teachers and I have managed individual conferencing with class sizes ranging from twenty to thirty-five children. It takes time to organize, so be patient.

The time you can allot for each conference depends on class size and the time you have for reading. Schools vary in their flexibility of scheduling. Obviously, teachers with children moving in and out of the room for special classes must deal with limited blocks of time. In our school, we tried different plans for creating time for conferencing. In addition to the minutes set aside for independent activities and conferencing, we planned some cooperative teaching to free even more time. Two of us worked together, planning thirty-minute activities for the combined two classes. This allowed one of us additional time for conferencing. After two more teachers joined the Language Experience crew, we alternated taking all four classes as a group, releasing the other three to work with individuals.

Introducing Conferencing

When I introduced Practice Reading, I also explained conferencing:

1. Every child was to have time alone with me. During this time I would listen to him or her read.
2. The conference could not be interrupted.
3. Each child would choose a day for his or her conference.
4. The child's name would be posted on a chart for that chosen day.

Monday	Tuesday	Wednesday	Thursday	Friday
Tony	Juan	Mathew	Kirsten	Elisabeth
Elissa	Anna	Toshiko	Irene	Gino
Kasha	Scott	Jay	Maria	Noburu
Eric	Kristine	Timmy	Gregg	Dolores
Mei	John	Mark	Susumu	Gail

5. The child was to read from the book used in Practice Reading.
6. Once an entire book had been used for a conference, it could not be repeated. All of the books in the room were listed on a ditto master and copies of the list given to each child. Once a book was completed, it was recorded on the child's book list as well as on my weekly conferencing sheet.
7. Conferencing was to be a binding commitment.
8. Children not conferencing were to "take care of themselves." Each person had something to do—and that was that. Tell the children exactly what you expect from them and exactly what they can expect from you.

At the beginning of the conference, the child tells about the story he or she is reading, and is asked either to read those pages that have been practiced or, if the book (or books) is finished, to choose favorite parts of the story to read.

During the oral reading of conferencing, the teacher assesses the child's application of word recognition skills, fluency of reading, and expression in reading. A conferencing sheet provides a running record of student progress, and is used to record your evaluation and diagnosis of the student's progress. At this time you may also introduce new skills to be learned. Use the time according to you and your student's needs.

Date	Pages	Book	Comments

Individual conferences provide invaluable information about each child. Close communication between you and each child is established. You will learn more in those 5 to 10 minute sessions than you would in daily sessions with round-robin reading groups. Some students read mammoth amounts of books and will want extra conferencing time. Still other children read less but want more reading time. In order to meet these needs you can have children read into a recorder and make tapes that can be played after school when you are relaxing.

However you decide to organize your conferencing time, working with other teachers or working on your own, you need to reserve at least a total of 25 to 50 minutes each day for listening to children read. It is time well spent. The information you have collected and recorded about each child will be invaluable at report card time and for parent-teacher conferences.

Organizing for Instruction

The class may be grouped according to the four organizational-procedures strategies. One group of children may need repeated experiences with basic sight words. Naturally, this group would also be those for whom resource people could be used, since the children will need to be told the unfamiliar words as soon as these are encountered. Reading material can be Language Experience stories as well as trade books or basal readers that present those words in context. If you have used self-selection for Practice Reading books, you may want to supplement group lessons with books that have more strictly controlled vocabularies. Another group of children may need practice using context clues, while yet another group can receive instruction in the use of sound/spelling patterns. A fourth group may be using a combination of all three of the preceding strategies. Groups would be temporary; they are suggested because it may help make individualizing more manageable for you.

Teachers planning to use small-group instruction during Practice Reading will have to give clear directions to the children who will work independently. They will need to know what to do if they encounter a word they do not know. This will depend upon the word recognition skills they are developing. You will also need to tell them what they should do if they finish reading while you are working with a small group. (Again, Chapter 8 will help you organize for independent learning.)

Small-group instruction with each group would be staggered. An organizational procedure you could use might be the following:

ORGANIZATION OF SMALL GROUPS
DURING 15–30 MINUTES OF PRACTICE READING

Monday	Tuesday	Wednesday	Thursday	Friday
whole class	group A with teacher	group B with teacher	group C with teacher	whole class
Practice Reading	group B independent	group A independent	group A independent	Practice Reading
teacher circulates around room	group C independent	group C independent	group B independent	teacher circulates around room

Three groups: Group A needs work with sight words.
Group B is working with context clues.
Group C is working with phonics.
Individuals are using all these strategies independently.

Room arrangement also needs to be considered in order to control noise factors.

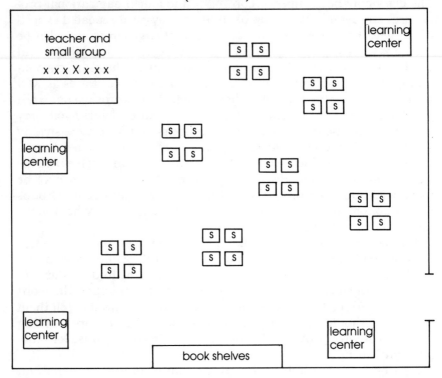

If you use resource people, they would be expected to guide children in applying their word recognition strategies. The teacher must take the responsibility to clearly and precisely instruct these aides that they are to focus the children's attention on the application of word recognition skills.

Resources for Reading Materials

Providing printed materials for children to read requires a good supply of books. That sounds simple, but with reduced school budgets we all know that buying *anything* is not simple. To begin with, you need to identify sources for finding books to buy. Basal readers can be used in an individualized reading program. Instead of having children read one story within a designated time, basals can be used as a collection of short stories with children choosing the number and order of stories they will read.

Providing a variety of basal readers should not be difficult. School districts sometimes receive complete reading series sets from publishing companies. Administrators usually store these books at the district office. Go to the district reading specialist or to the district curriculum library, look at the books, and check out the ones you want. Be firm! Those books should be in the classroom where children can use them.

In addition to basal readers, you can buy trade books (library books) for reading materials. Publishing companies will send free copies of their book catalogs. The following companies are particularly good resources:

Addison-Wesley Publishing Company
2725 Sand Hill Road
Menlo Park, California 94025

(*The Children's Language Program* includes 12 superb books. Be sure to examine the *School Catalog, K-8* carefully.)

Miller-Brody/Newbery
342 Madison Ave. Dept. 77
New York, New York 10017

Bowmar
P.O. Box 39247-A
Los Angeles, California 90039

Cartel
Dissemination and Assessment
Center for Bilingual Education
6504 Tracor Lane
Austin, Texas 78721

(annotated bibliography of bilingual materials)

Argus Communications
One DLM Park
Allen, Texas 75002

(focuses on self-awareness and cultural literacy)

Weston Woods
Weston Court
Weston, Connecticut 06883

(multicultural materials, including films)

Harper and Row Publishers
10 E. 53rd Street
New York, N.Y. 10022

(publishers of *Early I Can Read* and *I Can Read* books—great favorites of children. Migrant Education Service Centers often have these books in multiple copies.

Scholastic Magazines, Inc.
904 Sylvan Avenue
Englewood Cliffs, N.J. 07632

(annotated list of several hundred paperback books—includes general grade levels)

Holt, Rinehart and Winston, Inc.
383 Madison Ave.
New York, N.Y. 10017

(many of their books have accompanying tapes)

Follett Publishing Company
1010 W. Washington Blvd.
Chicago, Ill. 60607

Lollipop Power, Inc.
P.O. Box 1171
Chapel Hill, N.C. 27514

(a feminist collective that publishes excellent, inexpensive books. Some are bilingual.)

Harcourt Brace Jovanovich
757 Third Ave.
New York, New York 10017

(The ODYSSEY literature program is stunning.)

Anti-Defamation League of B'Nai
B'Rith   315 Lexington Ave.
New York, N.Y. 10016

(offers free bibliographies of children's books)

Interracial Books for Children
1841 Broadway
New York, N.Y. 10023

(their publications are not free)

Each year the International Reading Association publishes *Children Choices for 19—*. These are books children (K-12) have read, evaluated, and chosen as their favorites. Reprints of this publication can be ordered by writing:

IRA
800 Barksdale Road
P.O. Box 8139
Newark, Del. 19711

Although this is only a partial listing of resources, it should give you a starting point for ordering books.

Getting Money to Buy Books

There are ways to get money to buy trade books. One of my principals, Mr. Corner (an administrator who put children first), allowed me to use monies allotted for buying basal readers and expendable workbooks to order and pay for trade books. That might work for you. You can also ask for money from Parent-Teacher organizational fund-raisers. Children in your class can plan ways to earn money to buy books (my classes put together and sold collections of their Language Experience stories). Used book stores, public library used books sales, and garage sales provide limited sources of books.

Collecting books is a slow, but rewarding process. Your goal is to gather enough books over the year, each year, to form a solid supply of books for individualized reading.

Language Experience Lessons: Children with Special Needs

Children who experience difficulty in learning to read often become bored and discouraged with the endless routine of drill, yet they are also the children who need repetition. On the one hand, we realize that some children need to move slowly and repeat experiences with skill development; on the other hand, we must tie that skill to immediate use in reading for meaning and maintaining interest in the lessons. The activities that follow are designed to provide additional experiences while stimulating interest in the learners.

LESSON 1: Sight Words

As previously mentioned, sight words are high-frequency words used repeatedly in our writing. The sight word lessons suggested for beginning readers and writers in Chapter 5 and the lessons suggested for children with special needs, combined with the writing the children have been doing throughout the year, provide experiences with sight words in context. *These* lessons offer repeated practice with sight words in isolation. (Note that experience with words in context precedes experiences with those words in isolation.)

This is a game children have fun playing. It is an individual game called, *See It, Say It, Match It.*

The individual child plays the game by drawing a word card from a stack of cards, looking at it, saying it, and matching it with the word on the game board. When constructing these games I code them to indicate whether the words are from pre-primer, primer, first, second, or third grade books. The buddy system can be used with one child as the player, the other child as the checker.

A fellow teacher designed this game board and made several copies for our rooms. She color-coded the flower cards according to reading level.

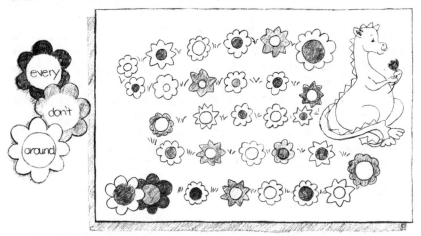

In the game, children draw a flower card, read the name, move their marker one space, and keep the flower card. If unable to read the word, they return it to the stack and draw another word. At the end of the game, children read their collection of words to the teacher.

Games such as these can be decorated with stickers from sticker fun books (or you can decorate the games with your own drawings). All games should either be laminated or covered on both sides with clear contact paper to protect them against wear and tear.

LESSON 2: Spelling/Sound Patterns (Phonics)

As mentioned before, some children need repeated experience if some skills are to become firmly fixed. Repeated practice with initial consonants, phonograms, consonant clusters, and phonics generalizations (such as the consonant/vowel/consonant or consonant/vowel/consonant/vowel generalizations) should combine auditory, visual, kinesthetic, and tactile experiences. The following suggestions can be adapted for use in practicing all of these spelling/sound patterns.

You will need sets of cards for both the teacher (whether this will be you, a buddy, an aide or a volunteer) and the child or children. The object of the activity is to have children learn to identify initial consonants within the context of a word. It is a simple, matching activity. Words representing the spelling/sound pattern are printed on no more than three to five cards. Children can be confused by more than that at one time.

If you are teaching initial consonants or consonant clusters, highlight them by underlining or coloring. The children place their cards plainly visible across their desks. The teacher holds up one of the cards and points to the initial consonant. It is crucial to carefully monitor your instructional language. Use consistent language in working with children. Do not continually reword instructions, but rather decide upon clear, simple words and then stick to them. When you vary your language even slightly for the same activity, children must pause to decide if you want them to do the same thing or something different. Structure and discipline your speech. For example, "Look for this card [the mug card]. Point to this letter [indicate letter]. It is the first letter. It is *m*. The first sound is 'm.' The word is 'mug.' Show me the mug card. Point to the *m*."

At a more abstract and difficult level, the person working with the children pronounces a word representing the sound/spelling pattern and asks them to shape the initial sound with clay. Yet another approach is to make word cards using material such as felt, corduroy, or cotton. As you pronounce the word, children trace it with their fingers, saying the word.

Finally, in the learning sequence, children write a one- or two-line story using a word representing the spelling/sound pattern being worked with. You might say, "Now think of a word you like that begins with the same sound as the word 'momma.'" That word is printed on a card and then the child traces with the index finger and says the word. A story is dictated using the word ("This is my momma. She works"). If you use the word card approach, each child will have a collection of words representing each set of spelling/sound patterns taught. The cards can be used repeatedly for practice and review.

There are other simple games you can make that provide repeated practice with spelling/sound patterns. Small game boards can be constructed in this manner:

d	s
t	m

str	bl
sn	tr

ight	un
op	at

As you pronounce a word, children put a bean (or any marker) on the printed symbol matching that sound pattern.

Keep in mind that true assessment of learning occurs only if the children can apply what they are learning both in their independent reading and in their writing. During Practice Reading and as the children write, you must consistently urge the children to apply the skills being taught.

LESSON 3: Children with Special Needs: Practice Reading

Children who seem bogged down in reading may become frustrated without additional help in Practice Reading. Oftentimes, they need to hear the story first, so that they can get the meaning of the story and hear the flow and rhythm of the language before they begin to read. It is a good idea to tape record the story or stories children will be reading. You can then have the children:

1. listen to the story.
2. read along with the tape recording, pointing to the words as they hear and say them to insure correct sound/symbol correspondence.
3. read the story on their own.

Practice taping stories to pace your reading at a rate that sustains the movement of the story, yet does not exceed the child's ability to keep up.

Language Experience Lessons: Second Language Learners

A major concern for teachers of second language learners is teaching sound/spelling pattern relationships. Often the sounds being taught are difficult for the child to produce. At this point in the Language Experience sequence, children should have had many opportunities to work with the oral production of sound without being corrected, the emphasis being more on content than on form. Now there will be a subtle shift. For those children who continue to bump up against differences in sounds between first and second languages, teachers will conduct some specific instruction. However, this instruction is not aimed at uniformity of sound production, rather, it is to insure that the child makes the correct connection between sounds and symbols. There is a distinct difference. Standardization of sounds is impossible. The sounds I use in saying, "rain, cup, at, stop" are not the same sounds produced by teachers native to Texas, Maine, Boston, and Nebraska. Clearly, standard sounds, for vowels in particular, do not exist within the total teaching community. Hence, it seems contrary to common sense to require second language learners to reproduce exactly our own idea of what constitutes correct sounds.

Lessons suggested here will, instead, focus on clarifying the sound/spelling pattern relationships in English. This means that if children still have difficulty producing sounds distinctly, listen to them and show them the letters for the sounds they intend to approximate. You respond to intent by showing form. The Vietnamese child who says "dog" with a "th" is shown the printed "*d*-og" (either in dictation or in isolation). You would say, "Yes, that is a big dog." The child's attempt to articulate "d" interacts with your showing the letter "d" and saying, "dog." This interaction clarifies and reinforces the child's knowledge of the relationship between the sound and the symbol.

Lessons on Sight Words

The Language Experience lessons suggested in both Chapter 5 and this chapter provide sufficient experience with sight words.

Lessons on Sound/Spelling Patterns (Phonics)

At this point in the Language Experience sequence, second language learners should have developed the ability to look at American English as just another coding system. From their experiences with oral and written communication, they know that language can be manipulated. Lessons on sound/spelling patterns can be introduced by clearly stating that you want them to focus on specific sound/spelling patterns. These patterns would then be taught directly.

For example, if students are dropping final consonant sounds of final inflections (such as -s, -es, -ed, -ing), you teach those word endings in the direct context of their use. Your initial concern should be to determine if the children understand the function of endings such as -s, -es, -ing. Do this by showing them pictures of single and multiple objects and asking them to touch a picture showing two objects. If you determine that they do understand pluralization at the receptive level, you teach them the symbols for that pluralization.

> There is one box.
> There are four box - es.
>
> I see one girl.
> I see three girl - s.

For -ing and -ed verb endings, you can provide concrete experiences to illustrate what *is* happening as well as what *has* happened.

> Tony is walk - ing. (as Tony walks)
> Tony walk - ed. (after Tony sits down)

As you explain the functions of endings (to tell about something being done now and continuously, or something that was done but has stopped) you illustrate the printed symbol for that action.

Children who are second language learners should be integrated with the rest of the class now for general lessons on word recognition skills.

Work on Dialects and Phonics

It seems strange that after all these years, a controversy still rages surrounding the acceptance of dialects such as Southern dialects or Appalachian dialects. As in any teaching situation, your responsibility is to listen to and talk with your children. By listening to the meaning of the children's communication, you can determine if they understand the relationship between sound and form. For example, you say nothing if a child is reading and alters the text so that

The funny baby cried.

becomes

The funny baby she cried.

The child who alters printed Standard English by reading in dialect, tells you clearly that the child not only understands the text but is also able to put it in the child's own words. *Any child who transposes Standard English into dialect shows skill, not deficiency.*

By combining speaking, writing, and reading, you show children the symbols for sounds they may be deleting. Your concern should be that they know the meaning for a particular spelling pattern. This knowledge can exist independently of oral language production. In this sense, teaching children that "runnin" is printed or written as *running* teaches the deleted ending. Making this clear is not intended to change oral language, but rather to teach the actual, symbolic representation of an actual word.

Independent Writing for All Students: Beginning Learners

All of the skills learned in independent reading are practiced and reinforced in independent writing. Sight words learned in reading become words used in writing; spelling patterns, initial consonants, phonograms, consonant clusters, phonics generalizations, and sound patterns are applied as aids in writing. With some children, this is spontaneous; with others you will need to give specific instructions. As you present specific strategies in spelling/sound patterns in reading, you emphasize those same skills in writing lessons.

You can say, "Today we learned about the sounds for b, m, l, and c/k. When you write your stories, think of the sounds of the words you write. Start spelling words all by themselves. Let's try spelling together. What if you write about seeing a bubble?" Have volunteers spell 'I see a _____' (these three words will be in sight reading vocabularies). "Listen to the word, 'bubble.' The first sound you hear is 'b.' What is the first letter of the word 'bubble'? Right, *b*. This is how you can begin to spell the word. I see a b_____ . Some of you may want to write the word by yourselves. Sometimes you will spell a word, and it won't look the same as in a book. I want you to experiment learning to spell all by yourselves."

You are encouraging idiosyncratic spelling because it promotes independent writing, it is self-correcting, and it forces children to think about the sounds and symbols of their language. This kind of spelling *is transitional*. When children write for public reading they will be taught how to find the correct spelling for words.

Prepare the children by telling them not to worry about spelling when they write their stories for you and for each other. Everyone works together to become independent, and to find many different sources of information, not just teachers and books. Emphasize that when authors decide to give their stories to other people—people who are an audience and may not know you—it is necessary to make sure that the words you spell look like words in Practice Reading books, math books, and library books.

Most teachers have learned that administrators and the public are concerned about poor spelling. Self-correction seems so vague that we feel hesitant to depend on it in teaching spelling. But the process of self-correction is not unusual; we all self-correct at an almost unconscious level. Children do the same. A third grade boy began many of his stories with "Once a pond of time . . . ." One afternoon he was reading a book that began with, "Once upon a time," and made the connection between what he had thought he heard and what was actually written. From then on he wrote, "Once upon a time . . . ." (Although, frankly, in this case that change may not have been much of an improvement!)

Remember, you are encouraging children to hypothesize, to work with and test their knowledge of language. This experience will help them master reading and writing. It tells them that trying to work on their own is good; it is valued. The first independent steps in walking, talking, and eating are always supported and encouraged. If a child is unsteady or falls down while learning to walk, we do not always try to keep that child from falling down. We want the child to keep trying and practicing until the child gains confidence and becomes increasingly skilled. The analogy applies to writing and spelling. Each step brings the child closer to skilled performance.

LESSON 1: Letter Writing

Children can begin writing letters by writing to each other and to you. The teacher can introduce the form of informal letters by writing a letter to the class. The letter should either be written on chart paper or on an overhead transparency.

Read the letter with the children. Ask them if they know why people write letters. Allow time for discussion. You may stimulate talk by asking if everyone can use the telephone to talk to friends who live far away; how letters can be used to visit with friends; how letters can share what we think and how we feel. Lead the discussion into mail delivery and mailboxes and explain the differences between mail delivery in urban and suburban communities. Have the children make their own mailboxes out of shoe boxes, decorate them with designs, and print their names on them.

Ask the children to answer the letter you wrote to them. Remind them that you want them to practice spelling words by themselves.

LESSON 2: Letter Writing

Choose letter writing buddies in advance for each child so that every child will have a partner. Discuss to whom friendly letters could be written and what to write about. For example, children might write to a friend about games they like to play, people in their neighborhood, their pets, books they like to read, songs they like—anything that tells about themselves and shares their lives. After reviewing the form of a friendly letter, tell the children that you have a secret friend (or pen pal) for each of them. Whisper the name of the pen pal in each child's ear, or give them each a slip of paper with the name on it. Each child writes a letter to the pen pal (who is another child in class).

LESSON 3: Letter and Envelope Writing

You will need envelopes for the letters written by the children. Before the day starts, draw an envelope on chart paper and address the envelope as a letter to the class. At the beginning of the Language Experience lesson, explain the information that must go on the envelope. Have the children practice addressing envelopes on rectangles of scratch paper. Then give envelopes to the children for addressing and mailing letters to their secret pals. Collect the letters and deliver them to the childrens' mailboxes in the classroom when the children have gone.

LESSON 4: Additional Letter Writing

Children read their letters and answer them.

Written Reporting

Children have worked with oral reporting in Chapter 2. We are now going to pick up on and use that experience in independent writing.

LESSON 1: Reporting

A natural extension of the letter writing lessons is a field trip to the post office. If this seems impossible, ask a mail carrier to visit the class, or take the children to the district office to find out how mail is sent from the main office to the individual schools. Planning any lesson on writing reports should begin with oral discussion and oral reporting. Here is a step-by-step sequence:

1. Tell the children they should find out: what happens to letters after they are mailed; why envelopes have to be addressed a certain way; why zip codes have to be put on letters; what happens if a name or complete address is left off the envelope.
2. Tell them they will plan a field trip to the post office to find answers to these questions.
3. Outline any problem solving procedure they will have to use in planning and implementing the field trip.
   a. Deciding the primary problem, "What do we need to do to plan a field trip?" (Identifying the main idea or topic of the report).

b. How do we get the information we need?

c. What is important for us to ask? What do we need to know?

d. Where can we get the information? (As they identify the people they will need to talk with, they will also be practicing the oral language skills developed through the lessons in Chapter 2.)

e. Who will get answers for our questions?

f. When will we need this information?

g. Set a deadline for the oral reporting.

5. Assess the information to determine if you now are able to implement the field trip.

6. If necessary, collect the additional information.

7. Go on the field trip.

LESSON 2: Reporting

As a class, write a rough draft of a report on the field trip to the children's parents, telling the parents why and how the field trip was planned and what the children learned from it. Save this rough draft because it will be used to teach proofreading and editing.

Poetry

If we view poetry as a formal, intellectual art form, poetry will be difficult for us to teach and for children to enjoy. The lessons presented here are based on the idea that poetry speaks directly to the feelings, experiences, and knowledge of the reader. This form of communication often defies analysis. Children deserve free experiences with poetry, its humorous, sensitive, painful, joyous best. Poetry not only provides an additional channel for expression; it also joins poet and reader in direct, often tacit communication.

The lessons begin with rhymed verse and move to free, unrhymed verse. The children have worked with rhythm and rhyme in the lessons on Playing with Words. By building on existing knowledge, children can move from the known, predictable rhymed verse to the less-predictable, unrhymed verse.

It will be necessary to precede writing with daily readings of poetry. The April, 1979 issue of *Language Arts* has an article by Carol J. Fisher and Margaret A. Natarella that reports on a survey of first, second, and third grade student preferences in poetry. The research reported in this article could help you choose the poems to read. According to Fisher and Natarella, most children prefer poems with:

1. rhyme
2. rhythm
3. contemporary language
4. humor
5. children and animals as topics.

Collections of poetry abound. I suggest a few that are particularly successful with large and small groups of children:

There is No Rhyme for Silver. Eve Merriam. (Atheneum, 1962)

Catch a Little Rhyme. Eve Merriam. (Atheneum, 1970)

Beastly Boys and Ghastly Girls. William Cole. (World Publishing Co., 1964)

A Little Laughter. Katherine Love. (Thomas Y. Crowell Co., 1964)

Chicken Soup with Rice. Maurice Sendak. (Harper and Row, 1962)

School is Not a Missile Range. Norah Smaridge. (Abingdon, 1977)

Oh, Such Foolishness! Edited by William Cole. (J. B. Lippincott, 1978)

Poems Children Will Sit Still For. Compiled by Beatrice Schenk DeRegniers, Eva More, and Mary Michaels White. (Citation, 1969)

Piper, Pipe That Song Again! Edited by Nancy Larrick. (Random House, 1969)

The following are collections of poetry written by children.

Miracles, Poems by Children of the English-Speaking World. Edited by Richard Lewis. (Simon and Schuster, 1971)

Here I Am!, An Anthology of Poems Written by Young People in Some of America's Minority Groups. Edited by Virginia Olsen Baron (Dutton, 1969)

City Talk. Edited by Lee Bennett Hopkins. (F. Watts, 1970)

The Voice of the Children. Edited by June Jordan and Terri Bush, (Holt Rinehart and Winston, 1970)

My Shalom, My Peace. Edited by Zim Jacob, Uriel Ofek and Dov Vardi (The American Israel Pub. Co., 1976)

If you would like even further resources of poetry, you can refer to current books on children's literature.

Lessons on poetry, as stated before, begin with reading poetry. Although the first writing lessons on poetry will use rhyme, in your reading intersperse a few non-rhyming poems so that children become accustomed to hearing free verse. Before you begin reading the poems, show the book of poetry to the children. Point out the visual differences between prose and poetry. Poetry is not paragraphed, its form is line-by-line, and in most cases each line begins with a capital letter. Some poetry such as that written by e. e. cummings, flows, walks, skips, and crawls across the page in an independent manner. Some poets use word arrangements to illustrate their poems. Robert Froman uses a word-picture device in his books, *Seeing Things* (Crowell, 1974) and *Street Poems* (McCall, 1971).

As you read different poems to the children, you and they can begin to keep a list of the "feelings" of poetry. Poems do create and evoke feelings whether they make us feel happy, sad, lonely, comforted, surprised, thoughtful, etc. Poetry also gives that flash of recognition, that "Ah ha! Yes, that's right!" feeling. The children also need to realize that poetry uses words economically, the fewest number of words for the clearest possible picture. You can ask the children to "tell" the poem. This telling (paraphrasing) the poem illustrates the greater number of words used in plain talk compared with the fewer number of words used in poetic speech.

To impress children with the individual, personal nature of a poem, children can illustrate (paint, draw and color, make stitchery pictures, model clay, create a collage) a particularly vivid poem. (*City Talk, Beastly Boys and Ghastly Girls* provide vivid images.) As the class talks about and shares visual representations of the same poems, you can stress that while poetry stimulates feeling and creates a picture, people can feel different and see different pictures for the same poem—which is as it should be.

The language of poetry may or may not rhyme. But the words usually create a rhythm. You must avoid a sing-song "one TWO, one TWO, one TWO, one TWO" as you read to the children. They can feel the rhythm without distorting the meaning or sense of the author's message with exaggerated reading.

As you begin lessons on poetry, continue the daily readings.

LESSON 1

Introduce this lesson by putting on chart paper one or two short poems with strong rhythm and rhyming lines. After reading the poem with the class, bring out their work on "When I was One" and "Juba." Either ask them to find similarities between their writing and the lines of poetry, or simply show them the similarities. The commonalities are rhyme and rhythm. Tell the children that they did such a good job with "When I was One" and with "Juba" that you think they can write their own poems. Explain clearly that, while these first poems may rhyme, later they will write poems that do not rhyme.

This lesson should culminate with whole-class revew of rhythm. Children clap the rhythm and supply the rhyming words for simple rhyming couplets. You can use nursery rhymes, song-verse, or jump rope chants for a simple, easy beginning.

Teddy bear, Teddy bear, turn around,
Teddy bear, Teddy bear, ___ ___ ___ (a three clap/rhyming addition).

LESSON 2

The children should make up their own first lines of rhyming couplets. These should be listed on the board. As a class, read the lines and clap the rhythm. Each child can choose a line to use in creating a couplet. They can write their verse on construction paper and illustrate them on the same paper. Finished products are mounted at eye level of the children, so that they can read them.

LESSON 3

Have the children find and stand by their illustrated couplets. Everyone reads his or her writing.

LESSON 4

This lesson begins the transition from rhymed verse to free verse. Free verse does not rhyme, and may or may not have a consistent rhythm. It uses a few words to create vivid images, feelings, ideas. To begin a discussion about emotion, ask the children to think about all the things that make them happy. On the board write:

I am happy when _____ .

As the children talk about what makes them happy, write their words or phrases on the board. The class should be allowed ample time to discuss the fact that different things make different people feel happy. Tell the children you would like them to write a poem about what makes them happy. The lines in the poem may or may not rhyme.

LESSON 5

This lesson should expand children's descriptive language. Point out that poets use words to "paint" vivid pictures. The class is going to practice finding new words for old words. Ask the children to tell words that describe sizes of things and write these words on the board. (Typically they will be *big, little, fat, thin.*) Ask the children to find another way to describe *big.* Use these responses to make a list of words that exchange old, worn-out words for less-commonly used words. Your class may not be expected to use a thesaurus or dictionary during this exercise, but *you* should. Children need to see the functional use of these resources for reading and writing.

At a concrete level, children can identify objects that are big, little, fat, thin; and they can use these concrete referents to create similes or metaphors. Another concrete activity is to have the children work with different kinds of movement as you provide alternative labels for that movement. While a child runs, walks, crawls, wiggles, slithers, etc., you and the class can list words describing those movements. Encourage children to think of new ways to describe familiar actions. Again, the teacher is responsible for adding to vocabularies by providing synonyms. As the children are working with words, underscore the utility of the word lists for future writing.

LESSON 6

The lesson that follows requires one full class period for playing with bubbles, one for both playing with and observing bubbles as they are created and die and, on the third day, writing poems.

You will need one bottle of bubbles for each set of two children. Allot one day for play with the bubbles. Ask the children to see how many different sizes of bubbles they can make and how high they can make the bubbles go; in other words, have the children experiment and play with the bubbles.

On the second day print

Seeing Tasting Hearing Touching Smelling

as categories across the board. Before handing out the bottles of bubbles, ask the children to think about being a bubble in a bottle. "As you come out of the bottle and blow into the air, what would you see, taste, hear, touch, and smell?" Have the children play with bubbles, pretending to be a bubble. After a time, they should begin to tell you words that describe the bubble's response to the world.

On the third day, begin with bubble playing and re-read the words listed under the five categories, adding new words if and when they occur. At the end of the play and talk time, the children are ready to write their poems: "I am a Bubble" or any poem about bubbles. Completed poems should be typed and copies made for every child to put together as a small book of poetry.

The diversity of response will surprise you. These are samples of poems written by children in my class:

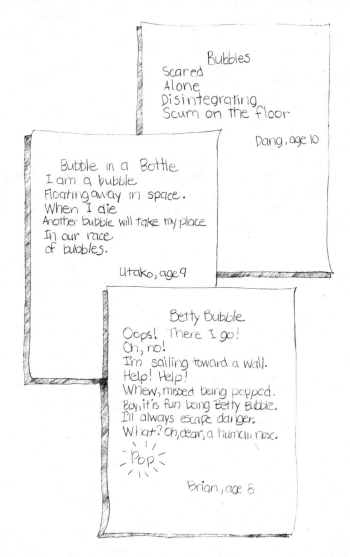

Bubbles
Scared
Alone
Disintegrating
Scum on the floor

Dang, age 10

Bubble in a Bottle
I am a bubble
Floating away in space.
When I die
Another bubble will take my place
In our race
of bubbles.

Utako, age 9

Betty Bubble
Oops! There I go!
Oh, no!
I'm sailing toward a wall.
Help! Help!
Whew, missed being popped.
Boy, it's fun being Betty Bubble.
I'll always escape danger.
What? Oh, dear, a human nose.
-Pop-

Brian, age 8

The bubble poems must be saved for lessons presented in Chapter 7, *Proofreading and Editing*.

Read poems written by other children (*Miracles, City Talk, The Voices of Children, Here I Am!*). Ask the children which poems they like best; how do they feel when they hear the poems? What do they see, smell, hear? Ask them to tell you what they think makes a good poem. As they give their criteria for a good (interesting, fun, etc.) poem, write those criteria on the board. Tell them that they have heard and read poems written by other children, and have seen books of children's poetry. Now you want them to make books of their own poetry. Children can either make individual books or work together in small groups putting together a collection of poems.

The poems should be saved for use in lessons on proofreading and writing.

Independent Reading and Writing for All Students: Intermediate Level

At the intermediate level, children with special needs, as well as children who are second language learners, should be totally mainstreamed. If they have progressed this far, special needs should have been met, and these children should require no more special instruction than other students. For example, if a second language learner has progressed through beginning level lessons in oral language to first stories, and then jumped to intermediate level lessons at Stage A in Independent Reading and Writing, this child can work independently within the total class without additional lessons.

The lessons on independent reading and writing use writing lessons to teach reading skills. Students who work with composing different mesages for different audiences for different purposes not only develop technical skills associated with public writing; they also develop expertise in reading those forms in print. Experience in writing fiction and nonfiction brings into conscious focus the ways in which authors of science, social studies, and math texts, pieces of fiction, and technical writing set about to communicate with their reading public. Writing becomes a shared craft; reading becomes shared knowledge.

We school teachers experience this kind of reciprocal learning. When we watch another teacher teaching, we recognize subtleties of communication between teacher and class that lay people may miss. What we see often serves to reinforce our own teaching techniques. A shared craft enchances perceptions.

The lessons in writing draw upon past Language Experience lessons. Lessons on oral language consciously build skills in communicating with different audiences, in different situations, for a variety of purposes. Continuity of purpose in learning experiences is sustained while moving toward technical skill using multiple forms.

Forms of Writing

The focus of functional writing will be based on that identified by Edna P. DeHaven in her book, *Teaching and Learning in the Language Arts* (De Haven. Boston: Little Brown and Co., 1979). De Haven's listed examples of functional (practical) writing is comprehensive. Whether or not you present the entire list to the class, you should introduce writing by having examples of a variety of published works on display in the classroom. Students should be given time to browse through the material which can be placed on one or more large tables. They can then compile a class list of practical, real life situations that require different kinds of functional writing skills. This will establish the purpose of the lessons that follow.

DeHaven's List for Functional Writing

Writing to describe or explain
the scene of an important event
a controversial or important personality
directions to a location
directions for playing a game
directions for making or doing something
how something works
opinion

Writing to record
diaries
journals
biographies of famous people
autobiographies
surveys
interviews and conversations
news stories
minutes of a meeting
subject area reports
book reports

Writing to convince
want ads
campaign literature
editorials

Writing as a social courtesy

  friendly letters

  invitations

  thank-you notes

  congratulatory notes

  letters of condolence

Developing proficiency in speaking necessitates knowing your audience as well as knowing how to code switch according to situation, participants, purpose, and form. Students also need to envision their reading audience in these initial lessons in functional writing. Some lessons require that students write for classmates; in other lessons they will write for a known audience, but one that may not share the writer's social or school experience.

LESSON 1: Writing to Describe

Description is not limited to any one writing form. But certain instances place stronger emphasis on the need for accurate description. In this lesson, student writing will be for a known, familiar audience. The lesson can either be introduced by listing all of the situations where people might need to describe what they see (you may refer back to the students' compilation of situations requiring functional writing) or you may use DeHaven's list. Some questions you might ask are:

"When would you need to describe an event?"

"When would you need to give a written description of a person?"

"When would you need to describe how to make something work?"

Next, students select a situation and purpose for writing and they identify the person in the room to whom they are writing. Their papers can give the following sort of information:

student's name:

situation:

purpose:

person to whom student is writing:

Do not provide specific directions concerning precision in writing. The descriptions they write for friends will be used to teach students why clarity in writing is important. They need to learn to distinguish between writing for people with shared experiences and writing for a general, often-unknown audience. (Elsasser and John-Steiner, "An

Interactionist Approach to Advancing Literacy" in *Harvard Educational Review*, August, 1977). We all must learn to "de-center" ourselves from the unconscious assumption that everyone knows what and about whom we are writing. This is as true for college professors as it is for fourth grade students.

When the descriptive papers are completed, students give their papers to the persons to whom they are written. As students read, they should use these guide questions:

1. Does the paper give enough information?
2. Do you have a clear picture of what was described?
3. Does the paper depend upon shared knowledge?

After the guided reading, discuss how knowing your audience and sharing experience with that audience affects your writing. Collect the papers and save them for Lesson 3.

LESSON 2

You will need to find examples of writing done for audiences with shared knowledge and shared experiences. They can be bulletins that the principal has written for teachers, newsletters from principal to parents, notes from teacher to teacher, PTSA notices, local newspapers, friendly letters, congratulatory notes, invitations, thank-you notes, minutes of a meeting, diaries, journals, etc. The class should spend three or four days reading samples of this material. (If you have limited resources, a page or two from either a diary or a journal can be duplicated.) The class should concentrate on analyzing the material to determine if it is explicit enough for audiences who do not share common knowledge with the author. They should also decide which situations dictate that audiences share knowledge with the author and which situations do not. They can categorize the forms of writing that can be used with a shared audience and draw upon oral language lessons that discuss distinguishing between formal and informal situations and between personal and impersonal audiences. Finally, discussion should focus on identifying reader responsibility. How carefully does one read an informal, personal piece of writing? Does one focus attention on form or content? Would formal impersonal writing require a different kind of reading set? How does the author's writing skill affect fluency in reading? Students should take notes on this discussion for use in future discussions on reading and writing.

LESSON 3

Students write a descriptive paragraph on the same topic they used in Lesson 1. This time, however, they write for an unknown, impersonal audience. Before writing begins, they should go over their notes from the last lesson, asking themselves or discussing as a class:

Can there be an assumption of shared knowledge?

What might that shared knowledge be?

What specific information does the audience need in order to have a clear picture of what is being described?

Are there certain phrases and words that writers should avoid (such as slang, local idioms)?

After the students have finished writing, return their first papers to them. Have them meet in small groups of four or five students to compare, discuss, and evaluate the significant differences between their first and second papers.

LESSON 4

Reproduce examples of student papers from Lessons 1 and 3. These papers should provide clear illustrations of significant changes in writing. Discuss the papers with the class and ask them what material they might expect to read that would require their close attention to detail. What writing skills could they use to make their writing easier for others to read? How would their authorship help them distinguish between effective writing and poor writing?

LESSON 5

Use your own judgment about the use of this lesson, but I believe it is our obligation to give students a pre-knowledge of the kinds of writing they can expect in testing situations.

You will need to develop a booklet of worksheets that replicate sample pages from standardized reading tests. Explain the uses of standardized testing to the students. Go through the booklet explaining what is meant by categories such as Word Recognition and Reading Comprehension. In small groups they should analyze and discuss each work page in the booklet. Guide questions could include:

Does the writing assume shared knowledge?

What is that shared knowledge?

Is the language clear or does it confuse?

What specific information does the writing give the reader?

Is it sufficient information?

What is the reader expected to do with the information?

The lesson may be extended to include previewing and analyzing math, social studies, and science tests. Students should conclude the lesson by drawing up a guideline for reading and understanding standardized tests.

LESSON 6

Other examples of standardized writing for an unknown audience should be collected for student analysis. These may include but not be limited to:

driver's manual

driver's test

standard forms used in doctor's offices, school offices, unemployment offices, and welfare offices; and mail order forms, rental agreements, and insurance forms

bus schedules

telephone books

classified ads

surveys

LESSON 7

Since students should have had time to browse through the materials on the writing tables and have read samples of different forms of writing that record information, they have enough shared experience to compile a class list of that record information. Now they may categorize the forms according to whether they can be used with both personal and impersonal audiences. Another specific dimension to be added is variety in language use. Because of their experiences with language as it is used on standardized forms, students have experience with formal and informal uses of language. As they decide whether or not a particular form (such as a diary) is formal or informal, personal or impersonal, they can also decide the kind of language that should be used with those forms. A chart such as the following can be developed:

FORMS OF RECORDING			
Language Use	Personal/Informal	Impersonal/Formal	Language Use
Conver-sation	a personal journal written by a woman attorney in 1946	Information from a standard doctor's form	Report-ing
discus-sion	a play with dialog between a mother and grandmother		

As students decide what goes where, they must supply reasons for their decisions.

LESSON 8

This lesson is totally open-ended. You and your class decide where the writing goes from here. Do they want to work on reporting, conducting surveys, writing a newspaper, writing editorials, or keeping individual or class journals? However you proceed, continuing emphasis should be placed on applying skills learned in writing to the reading of similar materials. Learning to write a formal report requires research, organization, anticipating one's audience, and planning a coherent, interesting presentation. Developing those skills in writing can be directly applied by students as they read and analize social studies and science books. Students become powerful readers and writers because they have worked with both process and product.

Assessment

Assessment of learning is built into the daily lessons at both the beginning and the intermediate levels. For example, by recording the individual application of word recognition skills during Practice Reading and during writing, you assess whether or not the children have learned what you have taught. When intermediate learners write using different forms of writing for different purposes and apply this knowledge in their reading, then you know they have developed knowledge through the information presented in the lessons. Your assessment should focus on whether or not the students are actually using the skills you have introduced and taught. For this purpose, you can use a checklist composed of the skills such as those listed at the beginning of this chapter. You can simply check off whether or not the student applies this learning to daily work.

Pertinent Resources

Atwood, A. *My Own Rhythm—an Approach to Haiku.* New York: Charles Scribner's Sons, 1973.

Cole, W. (selected by). *Oh, Such Foolishness.* New York: J. B. Lippincott Company, 1978.

Dee, R. *Glow Child.* New York: Joseph Okapaku Publishing Co., Inc., 1972.

DeHaven, E. P. *Teaching and Learning the Language Arts.* Boston: Little Brown and Company, 1979.

Dunning, S., Lueders, E., and Smith, H. (compiled by). *Reflections on a Gift of Watermelon Pickle . . and Other Modern Verse.* New York: Lothrop, Lee and Shepard Co., 1967.

Elsasser, N. and John-Steiner, V. "An Interactionist Approach to Advancing Literacy." Cambridge, MA: *Harvard Educational Review,* August, 1977.

Hoberman, M. A. *The Raucous Auk.* New York: The Viking Press, 1973.

Hughes, L. *Don't You Turn Back.* New York: Alfred A. Knopf, 1969.

Jordan, J., and Bush, T. (collectors). *The Voice of the Children.* New York: Holt, Rinehart and Winston, Inc., 1970.

Larrick, N. (selected by). *On City Streets.* New York: M. Evans and Company, 1968.

Maher, R. *Alice Yazzie's Year.* New York: Coward, McCann and Geoghegan, Inc., 1977.

Merriam, E. *It Doesn't Always Have to Rhyme.* New York: Atheneum, 1964.

——————— . *There is No Rhyme for Silver.* New York: Atheneum, 1962.

Morton, M. *The Moon is Like a Silver Sickle: A Celebration of Poetry by Russian Children.* New York: Simon and Schuster, 1972.

Roethke, T. *Dirty Dinky and Other Creatures.* New Jersey: Doubleday and Company, Inc., 1973.

Townley, Mary. *Another Look: Visual Awareness for Early Childhood.* Reading, MA: Addison-Wesley, 1978.

Zim, J., Ofek, U., and Vardi, D. *My Shalom My Peace Paintings and Poems by Jewish and Arab Children.* Tel Aviv: The American Israel Publishing Company, Ltd., and Sonol Israel, Ltd., 1976.

7

Proofreading and Editing

Student writing now goes public, and going public requires proofreading and editing. Students of all ability levels must participate in both the proofreading and the editing of their own material. Through this activity they learn the why and how of standard usage, spelling, and form. Because you have read to your students from the beginning and because they have come in daily contact with words in print (library books, newspapers, journals, magazines, content area books), they have seen why public form is necessary. Authorship for a general public is a familiar entity. Students know—from past experiences with oral language, reading, and writing—that if you want people to understand your message clearly and accurately, the form of the message must be clear and accurate. This is a common sense approach to teaching, using, and assessing basic skills.

As presented here, there is a distinct difference between proofreading and editing. Proofreading entails looking for and correcting errors in usage, punctuation, and spelling; it spotlights *form*, what some people consider the mechanics of writing. Editing concentrates on content. In this process the author asks if the material is reaching the audience and then screens for effectiveness of communication.

As you can see, we have given scrupulous attention to preparing children for this stage. They have had many Language Experience activities that stimulate expressive and receptive powers. Prior Language Experiences provided concrete situations where skills in writing and reading developed through direct application. We now bring these skills together with the student/author becoming a critical editor/proofreader of his or her own writing and the writing of other students.

Record Keeping

Record keeping serves more than one function. In addition to providing a visible charting of student progress through specific skills, it provides a tangible checklist for prewriting, writing and proofreading. Before the student begins composing the student knows what skills to keep in mind. There is no reason for creativity or thinking to be stifled by this disciplined organization.

There are at least three formats for record keeping, all in the form of checklists. The one you choose should directly reflect the focus of the current Language Experience lesson or series of lessons. For example, if the class is concentrating on mechanics, the list should include the specific skills you expect the students to apply, including those recently introduced and those already learned. In other words, beginning and intermediate level writers would be expected to use all of the skills introduced and practiced in previous lessons.

Another checklist might include only those items directly related to content—the effective use of language in communicating ideas, thoughts, information, and images.

A third option would be to create a balanced checklist that combines both form and content. But too much information at one time can be overwhelming, so it is suggested that this third option be used after students have had experience with other record-keeping checklists.

OPTION A

Student Name	Writer's Guide: Proofreading						
Language Experience Lesson	Capitalization	Spelling	Punctuation	Usage	Plurals	Word Order (sentences)
Short story #1	ok	needs to work on "ing" endings	good	excellent	excellent	try some deletions of over-used adjectives

Skills listed are determined by the competencies you expect.

Student Name	Edit for your audience: you want people to be interested!			
Language Experience Lesson	Organization of Ideas	Word Choice	Appropriate Audience	Captures Audience
Mosaic Poems	a fine combination of words to create ideas	great! vivid words	good focus	y<u>es</u>

This list should reflect those things that make writing interesting.

OPTION C

Student Name	Extra Aware Editing Perpetual Proofreading				
Language Experience Lesson	5 Senses (Word Choice)	Punctuation and Capitalization	Usage	Anticipated Audience	Spelling
My Family	☺	☺	☺	☹	☹
Favorite Things	☺	?	☺	☺	☺

Any balanced combination is possible.

Naturally, these samples are truncated and serve only to stimulate your own organizational abilities. The point is that the checklists provide:

1. a continuous record of student progress,
2. a basis for assessing student progress, and
3. a concrete referent for the student to use in disciplining writing.

Students need proofreading and/or editing checklists for reference before, while, and after they write.

The Process

Before they begin to write, it should be established that the students are expected to proofread their own stories. The teacher should give students checklists, so they can check off each conventional skill as they proofread their own papers. For instance, a student would go through the paper to correct spelling and then check that skill off on the checklist, and so on through punctuation, subject-verb agreement, etc., until every skill noted has been checked. The items on the list are determined by the teacher or by the teacher in conference with the class. If the school district has a basic-skills guide for your class's grade level, the checklist should include those skills; or the checklist could be based on the writing skills taught in the language arts text.

For students who are just beginning to write, the checklist should not be long. Proofreading is a time-consuming and laborious task, and the students should not feel unduly overwhelmed. Initial stories should be as short as one page and no longer than three pages. The more difficult the proofreading, the more quickly interest in writing and proofreading will vanish.

When students have proofread their own papers, they should take their stories to a junior editor (any other student) for that editor to proofread, using the same checklist and proofreading procedure as the author. After the junior editor has proofread the story, the author makes final corrections and revisions and takes the revised copy to the senior editor (the teacher) who goes over the story with the author using the checklist. This is also a time-consuming process, but it is always time consuming to establish a new procedure. Once the procedure is established, the teacher and the student will be less dependent on the final teacher/student editing since most, if not all, errors should be corrected by the students.

Playing with Sentences: Manipulating Words, Phrases, and Clauses

The purpose of editing is to strengthen written expression, which requires that students understand that they can manipulate language in print. Students cannot be expected to refine their work without first having concrete experiences with manipulating words, phrases, and clauses. The lessons on playing with words provide these pre-editing, pre-proofreading experiences.

We must deal not only with development of specific skills but with developments about the nature of language; and concept development is encouraged by operating upon content (language) and by noting the relationship of change in form to change in meaning (Hutson, 1980).

The idea of playing with language is familiar to the students. Past Language Experience lessons (beginning with Chapter 3, "Playing with Words: Metalinguistic Awareness") have prepared children for experimenting with sentence structure. Students now will learn about options in expression by using this information to edit their written materials.

Language Experience Lessons: Beginning Learners

In her article, "Moving Language Around: Helping Students Become Aware of Language Structure" (Language Arts, September, 1980) Barbara Hutson identified four categories of operations in manipulating sentence structure. These include: *additions* (adding words, combining sentences, adding clauses); *deletions* (taking out words, phrases, clauses); *rearrangement* (rearranging word order, clauses); and *substitution* (substituting synonyms, antonyms, phrases). This is not mindless play because students consistently focus on the consequences—the results of their additions, deletions, rearrangements, and substitutions.

The lessons that follow are very general in outline. To begin with, children practice building simple sentences using:

Sentences will use plural subjects with plural verbs. Further operations may include: changing sentences by altering verb tense; using adjectives, adverbs, and direct objects; and changing statements to questions.

The suggestions presented provide guidelines only. Lessons should be modified according to the ability levels of the children. All of the lessons will use word, sentence, and phrase cards.

Separate subject and verb phrase cards and single word cards of adjectives and adverbs should be made. (Volunteers can help.) Some of the subject cards should include compound subjects.

Verb phrase cards should also provide a mixture of singular and plural verbs. Cards should be made for *is, was, were, had,* and *has.*

If the words are printed on a ditto master, complete sets of cards can be run off on sturdy material (such as tag board) and cut apart to give to each child. Measure precisely, and use a paper cutter to save time.

Words on these cards should not only include those familiar to the child, but should also include new, vocabulary-expanding words. For example, you may have:

but you should also have:

Introduce the lesson by reminding the children of their play with words ("When I was One," "Clap, Clap, Clap Your Hands," "Juba," as well as their riddles and "Knock! Knock!" jokes. Explain that they are now going to play with words in sentences because they are authors and they want to make their writing clear and interesting.

Read and hand out three or four subject cards, reminding the children that there is a "who" to most sentences. Hand out three or four verb phrase cards. Hold up a subject card and tell the children, "This card tells *who*" (Mary); hold up a verb card and say, "This card tells *what* Mary did" (ran). Put the cards together and say, "Mary ran."

Tell them to play with their cards. The combinations may vary; they need only to make sense.

After the children have had experience manipulating the cards, give them (perhaps even the next day) two or three adjective cards and adverb cards and ask them to use their *new* describing word cards to add to their sentence.

Through these experiences, children gain knowledge of the parts of sentences and expand their understanding of the relationship between word order and meaning.

Lessons on adding to simple sentences needn't be limited to subject, verb, adjectives and adverbs. Additions may also include the following:

1. Make a number of cards that, when put together, form several sentences. Have children practice combining them into one sentence. (Add "and" cards.)

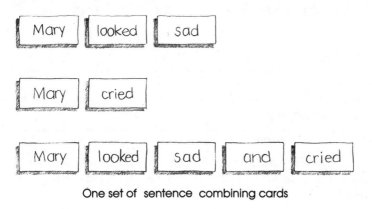

One set of sentence combining cards

2. Add cards naming objects of actions.

3. Add pronoun cards, including possessive pronouns.
4. Add "because," and "so" cards.
5. Add "why," "when," and "how" cards.

Children use these cards to create a large variety of sentences. The time spent depends upon the number of different parts of speech presented to the class. *All of the time* that children manipulate sentences through additions, you must focus discussion on what happens to the sentence when words are added. Does it make the sentence sound better? Do more words always tell us more? Do more words help us see a picture?

LESSON: Deletions

Deletions from sentences enable children to consciously work with the "meat" of a message—what the bare bones of the sentence are. For example, you do not absolutely need to know that Jesús is slow in order to know that he ran.

For these lessons, children first build simple sentences, to which they add adjectives. Then they take out any words not needed to tell who does what. The same procedure is used with adverbs. You may extend this lesson by adding and then deleting adjectives.

Again the emphasis is on discovering what happens to a sentence when we delete words; it is sometimes better to delete than to add. Children need to know that writing can be too wordy.

LESSON: Rearrangement

Beginning level students can work with creating nonsense sentences and then rearranging them.

Mother me kissed happy and was I.

By working with word order, you not only build a sense of sentence structure; you also vividly illustrate how closely meaning is tied to that word order.

LESSON: Substitution

Substitution brings into sharp focus the effects of word choice on interest, meaning, and impact of image. For this lesson make cards of antonyms and synonyms. Children first create sentences using words from either group, and then they substitute synonyms and antonyms. They should discuss the effects of the substitutions on the interest and meaning of the sentences.

Proofreading and Editing:
Beginning Learners

Manipulating sentence structure has prepared children for proof-reading and editing. They have concrete experience constructing sentences and then altering them with additions, deletions, rearrangements, and substitutions.

LESSON 1: Reports

In the first lesson the whole class works together. You will need Lesson 2: Reporting from Chapter 6 (page 159). The rough draft of the report on the field trip may be on large chart paper or on an overhead transparency.

With the class, prepare a checklist of skills relating to form, including:

1. My upper and lower case letters are good.
2. I capitalized the first letter of the first word of my sentences.
3. I put a period, question mark, or exclamation point at the end of every sentence.
4. I used complete sentences.
5. I spelled words correctly.

First, proofread the report, checking for everything on the list. (You may wish to make deliberate errors on the rough draft so that children can catch and correct them.) Then the class should edit. Now all of the operations come into play. Go through the report to see if it needs additions, deletions, rearrangements, or substitutions. Can the children use these operations to make their report more effective—more interesting to the intended audience, their parents?

LESSON 2: Letters

The children can write thank-you letters to the post office after their visit. Students will need to proofread using checklists and editing for clarity of expression. Since these letters are not exactly informal or personal, you may choose to introduce the business letter form at this point. Students should ask themselves, "Have I said what I want to say? Does the letter make sense?" I received a thank-you letter that never ceases to make me laugh. I have no idea if the little girl meant what she said!

Dear Professor Hansen-Krening,

Thanks for telling us what it is like to be a prof. I now have second thoughts.

Love, Melanie

In addition to the ambiguity of the message, Melanie actually was not with me long enough to know whether or not she loves me. This is not quibbling. Words used without discrimination become devalued. Children need to honor the meaning of words by choosing appropriate language for a given situation and audience. Although I treasure the letter and I want children to feel affection for teachers, I also hope that we can make children aware of the value of some expressions.

LESSON 3: Poetry

Poetry Lesson 7 in Chapter 6 (page 165) had children write poems that would be collected for a book of poetry. Now is their opportunity to use Hutson's four operations to edit their poetry. Since children had the option of working either individually or in small groups in composing the poetry, that alternative should extend to the editing process. You may design a checklist with the major headings that deal with addition, deletion, rearrangement, and substitution. You may also list subheadings.

Name(s):	Add	Take out	Rearrange	Substitute	Editor's Comments
Words					
Word pictures					
5 senses					
Ideas					

After editing their poetry, children may also proofread for legibility, spelling, punctuation, capitalization, and usage.

When junior editors have completed their work, the poetry comes to the teacher for final reading, after which the children make a final copy. These poems should be put in collections. Individuals and groups should design covers for their books. Some possibilities: put ink or thin paint onto paper and use a straw to blow the liquid into designs; tie dye covers; use melted crayon; cut and paste designs from books of wallpaper samples. Pictures of each student/author can be included on a title page or attached to the back cover of the book. Books may be shared with other classes and/or displayed for viewing and browsing in the school library. Some children may want to submit their poetry to certain magazines that accept submissions for possible publication, such as *Ebony Junior, The Electric Company,* and *Stone Soup.*

LESSON 4: Favorite Stories

Children simply choose a favorite Language Experience story for proofreading and editing. The checklist can combine skills related to form as well as specific points for editing (option 3 is an example of this integrated record-keeping device). The stories and their illustrations can either be put together as an anthology of short stories or put between individual covers as little books. The children should study trade books to determine how formally to list their names as authors and illustrators. They should also see several examples of dedications, which children do enjoy writing.

The books can be covered with contact paper to insure durability. If library card pockets are put on the inside of these covers and library cards inserted, the books are ready to be taken to the school library for anyone to check-out and read!

Language Experience Lessons: Intermediate Learners

Manipulating sentences develops powerful writers. Using additions, deletions, rearrangements, and substitutions helps students grasp how they can expand, clarify, and alter meaning by deliberately performing operations in written expression. Writing becomes a controlled, disciplined process.

Sentence frames help students develop an awareness of syntax and sentence parts. Students can make their own frames or pockets:

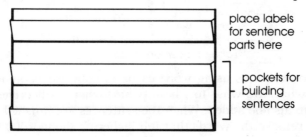

place labels for sentence parts here

pockets for building sentences

LESSON 1: Adding to Simple Sentences

Students construct all of the parts of this lesson. They will need at least 20 blank cards for sentence building, and sentence additions.

The "Who (What?)" card is placed at the top left of the frame. The "Does What?" card goes at the upper right side of the frame. Students then write one card that answers "Who?" and another answering "Does what?". Students build sentences by placing the word cards in the sentence frames. The purpose of the lesson is to teach the students to see the order of subjects, verbs, adjectives, and adverbs, and to experience the changes in meaning that occur with additions. Children who need a slower pace can spend one class period creating sentences, the next adding adjectives, the next adding adverbs, and the final periods adding both adjectives and adverbs. Work with verb tense can be extended if students make cards that read:

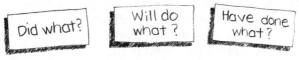

These cards are placed as labels for sentence parts.

Students build sentences by making verb cards that answer, "Did what?, Will do what?, Have done what?"

LESSON 2: Deletions

Students add a "To whom/What?" card and a "Where?" card to their collection of sentence parts.

Labels for sentence parts.

The lesson requires using word cards to compose sentences that tell: who (what) did what to whom (what) where. Adjectives and/or adverbs can also be added. When the sentences are finished, ask the student to remove the words that tell "where"; the word(s) that tell "to whom or what"; the words that describe "who (what)"; the words that describe "does what" (did what, will do what, have done what).

Class discussion centers on the ways deletions affect the clarity of the message; the ways deletions and additions help the reader understand the sense of the communication; when deletions should be used; and in which situations, for which audiences, and for what purposes bare bones sentences would be necessary.

LESSON 3: Rearrangements

The label card "Why?" is added to the cards labeling sentence parts.

Students build sentences that follow the structure of

```
              will                 what
Who (What)---► does what ---►to whom---►where ---►why.
              has done
              did
```

As you can see, a response to the "Why?" card introduces the use of clauses beginning with *although, because, since, so,* etc. Students build sentences following the above order and then practice rearranging the clauses within the sentence structure. Discussion revolves around the effects of the manipulation on interest, clarity, and impact of the sentence arrangements.

LESSON 4: Substitutions

In this last operation, students create sentences including as many parts or as few parts of a complete sentence as they choose. They exchange sentence frames with a buddy, who edits the sentence for clarity, interest, and effectiveness of message. If the buddy feels that additions, deletions, rearrangements, or substitutions need to be made, the buddy will indicate this, explaining the reason to the author.

A similar approach can be used in constructing paragraphs using paragraph frames or a worksheet. First the students identify the main idea for their paragraph. (What am I writing about? To whom am I writing? What do I want to say?) Then they develop a topic sentence for the paragraph (the opening statement) and practice developing written support for that statement. The written support explains why the statement was made and expands upon the topic sentence. Following this, students practice composing a concluding statement.

> **Statement:** *Hot lunch is expensive.*
> **Support:** *It costs $1.25.*
> **Conclusion:** *I can't afford to buy hot lunch.*

As you can see, this process lends itself well to functional writing. It also allows students to work with entire sentence additions, deletions, rearrangements, and substitutions within the broader framework of paragraphs. Certainly these experiences not only create more powerful writers, they also teach children about different kinds of functional writing. Working with the structure of a paragraph graphically illustrates where readers should look for topic sentences and for concluding statements. This is a crucial skill in skimming for pertinent information.

Working with supporting statements can expand from using opinion and personal experience to documentation from other sources. In these lessons, students learn to distinguish primary from secondary sources—a most important critical reading skill. Regardless of how you use lessons on the structure of functional writing, the key point is to relate these experiences with writing to similar experiences with reading.

LESSON 5: Creative Writing

Sentence play now needs direct application to either creative writing or functional writing. These Language Experience lessons focus on creative writing. (You can take the lessons from Chapter 6, functional writing and, on your own, develop them as lessons for proofreading and editing.) The students would consider their writing from the viewpoint of situation, audience, and form. Completed pieces would then be proofread for correct usage, spelling, punctuation, and capitalization. Editing would employ strengthening writing through additions, deletions, rearrangements, and substitutions.

Creative writing covers many different forms such as short stories, song lyrics, plays, and poetry. The following step-by-step procedure for story writing was developed by a marvelous classroom teacher, Eileen McMackin. She taught this unit to all of the 5th through 7th grade language arts classes in her school. Students who gave minimal effort to other lessons reversed their behavior when they became involved with Eileen's lessons. Interest was high and everyone took part.

OBJECTIVES FOR LANGUAGE ARTS UNIT ON STORY WRITING

Each student will have a folder. The left side of the folder will be used to keep work in progress. The right side will be used for completed work. On the right side students will also keep their evaluation checklists and their personal evaluation sheet.

Students will

1. Listen to a short story that has simple characters, setting, and plot, but high interest.
2. Tell what they think are the essential elements of a short story. (If they don't come up with them on their own, ask questions to bring out the elements of setting, character, plot, and meaning or theme.)
3. Listen to a good character description and discuss:
   a. What do you know about the character from listening to that description?
   b. What words give you clues to the character's physical appearance? to personality?
4. Listen to two or three more good character descriptions and continue listing key words on the board.
5. Make a short evaluative list of things they should include in a character sketch. List should include correct spelling, punctuation, word usage, and legibility.
6. Practice writing a brief character sketch. (Students can use a real

person that they know or a character from a movie they have recently seen or a photograph of someone whose characteristics show in facial expression or stance.)

7. Meet in small groups of four or five to evaluate each other's character sketch and give suggestions. Each student will record the group's concensus evaluation in the form of an O (needs improvement) or a checkmark (good) in the proper places on the evaluation sheet.

8. Revise and meet again with group; record evaluation; write final draft and place it in right side of folder with a star in the upper right hand corner (a clue to the teacher that this is a final draft). If necessary, teacher will conference with students who are having problems with their character sketches.

9. Listen to an example of a good setting description and discuss the importance of the setting coming out in a few key words and phrases in the beginning of the story. List on the board the words and phrases that gave this particular setting its time and place.

10. Listen to two or three more setting descriptions and continue listing on the board.

11. Make a short evaluative list of things that should be included in a setting description, including correct spelling, punctuation, usage, and legibility.

12. Practice writing a paragraph that describes a setting, using words that encompass feeling and mood.

13. Meet in evaluative groups to go over each other's setting descriptions. Students record group's evaluation on their sheet.

14. Revise and meet again with the group. Record evaluation. Write final copy and place it with a star on the right-hand corner in the right side of the folder.

15. Listen to a very short short story. Discuss the shape of the plot and the amount of time allotted to the beginning, climax, and ending of the story.

16. Define plot as a problem faced by a character and its solution. Both the problem and solution must suit the character and be worked through that character. The problem must be a difficult one.

17. Set up a list of possible plots by thinking of a character and adding a "What if . . ." situation. Example: Bill is the best player on his soccer team. What if Bill sprains his ankle on the day before the final play-offs?

18. Meet in evaluative groups and evaluate each other's plot starters on the basis of:
    a. Does the situation suit the character?
    b. Is there enough conflict to develop an entire story?

19. Listen to another short story. Using this as a basis, along with the other stories heard so far, write a possible story recipe.
    Example: Think of a character.
                What does this character want more than anything?
                What keeps this character from having what he wants?
                What does the character do to overcome the obstacle?
                What does this story mean?

20. Discuss how the recipe might be used in the following kinds of fiction short stories: fantasy, animal, realistic, science fiction, mystery.

21. Write a story using the recipe format. Be sure to plan the story before writing it.

22. Discuss what things to look for in revising a story and list them.
    Does the story have a beginning, highpoint, and ending?
    Is the problem hard enough?
    Is the character interesting?
    Have I used all five senses to create setting?
    Have I used punctuation correctly?
    Have I spelled words correctly?
    Is my writing clear and easy to read?
    Is my grammar correct?
    Have I included too much information?
    Have I left out anything important?
    Is the ending satisfying?
    Have I used my words well?
    Does the story sound good when I read it aloud?
    Is this the best job I am capable of doing?

23. Attach checklist to front of folder.

24. Meet in evaluative groups to read each others stories and offer suggestions. Each student should record suggestions made by his group on a piece of paper for later study. Record √ or O in appropriate places on evaluation sheet.

25. Have students read their own stories into a tape recorder and listen to the stories to see if they sound right.

26. Rewrite the stories using corrections and revisions where needed.

27. Conference with teacher to check revision.

28. When ready to write final copy, study a few books to see how the first page and title page might be done. Approximate the number of pages needed. Fold typing paper in half. Fold all the pages together and number them in order from beginning to end. Be sure to leave pages for illustration if you want them. Make title page. Make a lined and margined guide to hold under the typing paper while writing. Print story legibly. When finished, keep in folder.

29. Examine a number of book jackets to determine what information is on them.
    Cover: title, author, design or picture.
    Inside front: summary of story.
    Inside Back: continuation of summary and list of other books by same author.
    Back: Information about the author, picture of author.

30. Have a picture taken by a photographer if possible.

31. Design a book jacket for stories using colored paper, crayons, paint, letter stencils, and any other materials.

32. Discuss what information is included in the "About the Author" section.

33. Write down a list of questions to ask when interviewing an author.

34. Interview a classmate and write up the "About the Author" section for that person; exchange with partner.

35. Using interviewer's write-up fill in "About the Author" section about themselves; the student's picture can be pasted on the book.

36. Make a hard cover for the book; cover with book jacket.

37. Attach pages of story together by stapling or sewing, to form a binding.

38. Color-code bindings for kind of story it is: mystery, animal, fantasy, etc.

39. Exchange books for class reading.

40. In a concluding discussion, share what students like best about each book and share orally (by reading) the parts they think the whole class might enjoy.

Evaluation Sheet

NAME 0 = needs work √ = good				Group Comments	Teacher Comments
Character Sketch					
physical appearance					
personality					
spelling					
punctuation					
word usage					
Setting Description					
word choice					
5 senses					
spelling					
punctuation					
word usage					
Plot Starters					
suit character					
enough conflict					
Short Story					
shape					
problem					
interesting char.					
setting (5 senses)					
punctuation					
spelling					
usage (grammar)					
too much info.					
not enough info.					
anything left out					
satisfying ending					
word selection					

Prepared by Eileen McMackin

Students need Language Experiences with a variety of poems written by many different authors to show them the diversity of poetry. This is necessary because the word *poem* sometimes evokes groans (which may be for the benefit of their peers). Such a reaction is often the result of years of exposure to adult-selected poems on adult-selected topics, given like doses of castor oil. This is nonsense. All children, regardless of their life experiences, can find delight, solace, revelation, and confirmation in poetry.

Students need time to browse through collections of poetry written both by adults and by boys and girls of their general age. Studies that have determined student preferences in poetry can help you make selections. Many intermediate students like poetry that rhymes, is humorous, uses contemporary language, is a narrative, and uses familiar experiences in the content. Material should not be limited to these characteristics because tastes vary. If you provide a variety, students can choose what they like. Ask the students to jot down their own choices and then read those self-selected poems to the entire class. Children should have extensive experience with this literary form so that they become familiar with the sounds of rhyme and rhythm.

To introduce poetry writing, lead the class in a discussion on: Why and when do people write poetry? How can you distinguish between a poem and a story? How do you write a poem? Show the children how to write a class anthology of poetry. As examples, show the class:

> *The Voice of the Children.* Edited by June Jordan and Terri Bush. (Holt, Rinehart and Winston, 1970.)
> . . . *I Never Saw Another Butterfly, Children's Drawings and Poems from Terezin Concentration Camp.* (McGraw-Hill Book Company, 1962). (Pay particular attention to the "Catalogue of Poems." It tells how the poems were collected, when they were written, and brief statements about the fate—if known—of the author.)

The books should not be shown as models, but to stimulate the interest of the class and to show students that young people can and do write poetry.

LESSON 1: Preparing

Any writing, poetry in particular, necessitates having command of a wide range of descriptive words and phrases. There are at least two approaches to developing a repertoire of descriptive language. The following chart exemplifies one approach:

Hearing	Seeing	Tasting	Smelling	Feeling
bang! bang! zing!	snaggle-tooth	sour pucker	burning Sunday roast	kitten-fur

Such a chart can be mounted in the room. Choose some poems that use descriptive language related to the five senses. As you or the class reads the poems, list words and phrases that evoke strong images.

Another chart, focusing on feelings, suggests a second approach:

Happi-ness	Fear	Sor-row	Love	Peace	Despair	Frustra-tion	anger
	Sol-dier's hearse	empty		dove	hunched old woman	steal, ask + ask	

The charts are used for the next lesson.

LESSON 2: Mosaic Poems

In small groups or individually, as they prefer, students choose topics (such as fear, hunger, play, eating) for writing. Words and phrases relating to each topic are listed and are then put together as a poem.

The authors go through the poem, editing (using additions, deletions, rearrangements, and substitutions) and proofreading. Edited copy can be illustrated through collaborative art work, collages, or murals, and mounted to be placed in the room, in the hall, in the lunchroom, or in any public place.

Cinquain gives structure of form while stimulating creative expression. The structure of cinquain is

One word

Two adjectives

Three action words

Four word statement about topic

Synonym or adjective for first word

> Stars
> Brilliant, bright
> Dance, zoom, twirl
> Encompass my soul wordlessly
> Companions
> by Elizabeth

Individuals can choose their own topic for cinquains. Once rough drafts are completed, they can be typed on a ditto master, duplicated, and distributed for proofreading and editing. Take a picture of each author and have the students write autobiographical sketches to go with them. Mount pictures and autobiographies so that they can be reproduced as an afterword to the poetry books. Edited copy is reproduced, pages collated, afterwords added, and covers made and attached. Completed books can be distributed to other classes, other schools, parents, and school and/or public libraries.

Assessment

Assessment begins with the first lesson and ends with the last lesson. It is a continuous process through proofreading and editing. The teacher's role is to participate in the student assessment, keeping a master sheet or record that notes each student's progress. The combination of teacher record keeping as well as the student's own record keeping provides written documentation for report cards and parent conferences.

Concluding Thoughts

If you have followed the cyclic development of Language Experience, you now live with the excitement and fascination of autonomous, self-disciplined, powerful communicators. All of the students have gained control (in varying degrees, of course) over their abilities to read and write with comprehension and deliberation. Assessment becomes an active, context-specific process, just as learning has continued to be dynamic and valued by your students.

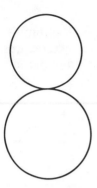

Organizing

Organization makes the difference between purposeful self-direction and a milling mass of students. I will present, from my experience and the experience of other Language Experience Approach teachers, what are the three most important components of room organization:

1. Anticipating and channeling student behavior.
2. Providing materials for learning.
3. Room arrangements for maximum space and minimum confusion.

In my opinion, thoughtful, well-planned organization determines the success or failure of any reading/language arts program. But being able to develop independent thinkers and movers becomes even more crucial in a Language Experience classroom. Valuing and respecting oneself and others is an integral part of both Language Experience and of channeling one's own behavior (or, as my first graders usually said, "taking care of yourself").

Of course, teachers must set up their classrooms according to their own philosophies. Some people feel reluctant to entrust any responsibility to children while others operate at the other end of the spectrum and give full responsibility to children. I tend to operate between these two extremes. My tolerance for noise and confusion is limited; consequently my attitude toward acceptable behavior will reflect this. You, in turn, know the extent of your own flexibility and must use that information in assessing and choosing from my suggestions.

Anticipating and Channeling
Student Behaviors

Anticipating behavior problems is stopping trouble before it begins. Anticipating behavior means that the teacher *observes* the students and their individual personalities; *considers* the situations in which these personalities will be placed; *evaluates* the probable interaction of personality and situation; and then *plans* to avoid any negative interaction between environment and student. This sounds more involved than it actually is.

For example, you might want to introduce a bingo game to a group of fifth graders. Watching your fifth grade student, Anne, on the playground, in the lunchroom and in the halls, you discover that Anne likes to throw things—pellets of bread, pieces of eraser, anything small enough to aim and toss. You realize that the bingo game you plan to use in class (bingo uses small markers) would pose an irresistable challenge to Anne. You also realize that the informal atmosphere of bingo games creates a general excitement which might make it even more difficult for Anne to contain herself. You have already used the first three steps: *observation* of individual personalities; *consideration* of situation; and anticipation of the *interaction* of personality and situation. You have anticipated possible behavior. Some techniques you might use to stop trouble before it begins include:

1. Have the class make the rules for playing bingo. This can be done quickly and it removes the teacher from the role of disciplinarian. It requires that children anticipate the consequences of their own behavior, while developing problem solving skills.
2. Stand by Anne's desk while calling out the words, letters or numbers. This often works as nonverbal prevention.
3. Should Anne start to throw the marker, you can calmly and matter of factly put her arm or hand down.
4. If all else fails remove all the markers from her desk with no comment, totally ignoring any outraged protest. She knows perfectly well why you are doing this.

Several lessons in this book involve a definite break with school routine (interviews, field trips). This requires anticipating problems that might arise. Often times children "misbehave" simply because they don't know what *is* appropriate. They have no pre-established guidelines to follow. Additionally, many children have never been taught to consider consequences that follow action. For instance, there was a principal (my mother) of a school in an unusually wealthy neighborhood who had *assumed* that because parents spoke frequently of family "cultural" excursions, their children knew how to behave in places such as art museums, theaters, and concert halls. The sixth grade class from this school went on a field trip to a local art museum where they distinguished themselves by shoving adults and children around, shouting across rooms at each other and capping things off by having a pop-squirting fight in the lobby. The curator of the museum called the principal and invited the school to stay away from the museum. My mother held a class meeting with the students, the majority of whom were amazed that anyone had thought that they had been irresponsible and rowdy. During this meeting an important fact emerged; many of the children did not understand that in some situations certain kinds of behavior not only infringe upon the rights of others but also may result in destroyed property. The intent was not malicious; it was thoughtless and ignorant.

With any group of children, planning for a new or unusual experience should begin with clearly defined expectations for individual and group behavior. Once the class definitely understands what is expected, deviations from those expectations should result in one of two consequences: (1) the student is removed from the situation; (2) the student is not allowed to participate in a similar experience in the future. Students need to learn that the choice is theirs and the consequences which follow those choices are also theirs.

Role playing provides important information in preparing a class to participate in new experiences. It helps students anticipate. It has been used with equal success by teachers in all of the elementary grades. Role playing meets purposes as diverse as preparing first graders for their first day in going through a hot lunch line to a fourth grade class preparing to interview the principal or librarian. Role playing involves identifying the situation, the participants, and the purpose. In doing this, the students become familiar with whether they are dealing with a formal or informal context and what actions are expected of them. After the first role playing, the students can discuss and evaluate what has happened. They may decide to repeat the role-playing process with modifications in the behavior of the actors. In any event, they have proceeded through the entire interaction and have seen, in actual fact, the consequences of those actions. In *Role-Playing for Social Values*, Shaftel and Shaftel state, "When young people explore in action the consequences of choices they have made, they can more easily see causal relationships. . . . Children can be helped to see that (1) behavior is caused, (2) it occurs in a setting, and (3) there are usually multiple causes for behavior." (Shaftel, F. and G. Shaftel. Englewood Cliffs; Prentice-Hall, 1967)

Furthermore, role playing often relieves the unvoiced anxiety people feel when they face new experiences. Typically, individuals do not act like themselves when they find themselves on unfamiliar ground. Some people become withdrawn and quiet while others cover up their feelings with loud voices and bravado. Most of us have said to ourselves, "Now why did I act like that? That's not what I usually do!" Even those who appear completely calm are often covering up anxious feelings.

"How could you look so calm? I was a nervous wreck!"

"Boy, you sure did that well."

"Who, me? I was scared to death!"

"Well, you sure didn't look like it!"

Going over the problems (how to act in a new situation) and establishing guidelines and expectations for actions will help students know just what is expected of them. Once they know what is expected, most of their apprehensions will be eliminated, and their actions will be more normal and they will feel more at ease.

Reading Nonverbal Cues

During the role-playing process, the children should also be taught to read nonverbal cues in both the setting and the body language of their fellow actors. (This ties in with the lessons in Chapter 2.) Learning to read nonverbal cues is an essential survival skill which is often left for the child to develop by trial and error. The importance of learning nonverbal skills quickly becomes clear when you stop to consider the many times the following thoughts have crossed your mind, "Not now, why can't they see that I'm in no mood to discuss this now?" or, "Why can't they just leave me alone? I am much too busy to stop and talk to them now," or "No, this is neither the time nor the place. . . ." The examples are obvious for teachers but less obvious to students. Consider the times children have given their teacher lunch money while the teacher is busy. Later they come to the teacher and ask for the money. The teacher looks blank and says, "I don't remember your giving me any money." The students stand speechless and may even look outraged. "We did too give you our lunch money." In this instance, if the students involved had read the teacher's nonverbal cues, they would have known that the teacher was too busy to pay attention and the problem would have been avoided. As stated before, this type of decoding cannot be left to incidental learning. Out of school, children may have learned to read parent and sibling cues, but they haven't learned to read school cues.

Teachers can teach children to read nonverbal communication by adding the following types of questions to the role-playing process:

1. How do you read body language and facial expressions? ("How did the teacher look when you were talking?")
2. How do you determine whether or not the timing is right? ("What was the teacher doing at that time?")
3. How do you decide whether or not the place is right? ("Was the teacher collecting lunch money then?")

There are many role-playing possibilities available for practice in reading both teacher and peer nonverbal cues. For instance, the students could role play this hypothetical situation:

Tony races out on the playground to play basketball with Roosevelt and Lee. When he gets to the basketball court, he sees that Lee is sitting with his back against the pole. This surprises Tony because Lee is always shooting baskets the minute he gets on the court.

What would be the consequences if Tony did not consider the situation and try to read Lee's nonverbal cues? Each of the foregoing examples help children and teachers learn to anticipate and channel behavior.

A Shared Responsibility

The ultimate goal for the teacher is to communicate the need to *share* responsibility for anticipating and channeling behavior. By beginning the year with defining class rules, many problems can be anticipated and eliminated before they occur. As the year progresses, more and more responsibility shifts from the teacher to the students. Achieving this shift is accomplished through class meetings and role playing.

Responsibility is learned only by evaluating the situation and choosing a path that a person thinks will be more helpful to him/herself and others. Given an opportunity to learn this from kindergarten onward, children can become responsible and socially aware; we will need fewer rules and punishments. . . . Children need teachers who will encourage them to make a value judgment of their behavior rather than preach or dictate; teachers who will help them plan better behavior and who will expect a commitment from the students that they will do what they have planned. They need teachers who *will not* excuse them when they fail their commitments, but *will* work with them again and again as they commit and recommit until they finally learn to fulfill a commitment. When they *learn* to do so, they are no longer lonely: they gain maturity, respect, love and a successful identity. (Glasser, W. *Schools Without Failure*. New York: Harper and Row, 1969)

Techniques for Developing Self-Control: Intermediate Grades

Intermediate grade students are, as a rule, socialized to the belief that teachers are either "tough" or "easy." If a teacher is tough, students know that they are supposed to keep their mouths shut and do the assigned work. If a teacher is "easy," students plan to establish a reign of anarchy.

Admittedly, this presents an "either/or" situation which eliminates or ignores the middle ground. But it does illustrate that the older the student, the firmer, the more strongly established are the patterned expectations about the way teachers and schools are supposed to be. Intermediate grade boys and girls have been socialized to expect teachers to behave in specific and consistent ways. These expectations make it more difficult for teachers to establish a classroom where *students* make a commitment to control and determine their own behavior. Consequently, if a teacher begins the school year by removing all established rules, students are often bewildered. Not having had experiences with self-direction and choices, they are ill-equipped to suddenly assume those responsibilities. All people, whether adult or child, experience feelings of anxiety, confusion, and uneasiness when precipitated into a world that has no guidelines.

This reluctance to assume a decision-making role may be even greater with children whose culture defines the teacher's role as one of absolute authority. Some children expect the teacher to be in total control. To ask them to jump right in and share in decision-making is unfair and unreasonable. The children may be so confused that their actions become withdrawn or totally out of bounds. Caution and sensitivity to a student's past experiences should be used to avoid overwhelming any group of students.

One of John Holt's books exploded on the teachers of one school district via an administrator who had more enthusiasm than common sense. After reading the book, this fellow decided that on the following Friday his elementary school would have "John Holt Day." All teachers were to give control and decision-making to their students. There was no discussion of this decision and its implications for the school day with the teachers. It was a decree. The administrator decided that if on this day the students controlled themselves and their classes with democratic, mature judgment, it would prove that John Holt was "right." If the day failed, self-direction in students would have been proven to be an impossibility, a myth pushed on educators by impractical radicals. Needless to say, the day was a complete failure—and, unfortunately for the teachers and the children, it was not even a dismal failure. It was a *rousing*, chaotic failure. Some enterprising students left school, some threw books out of windows and some sat in a state of shock. The only surprise about "John Holt Day" was that anyone survived! The principal retreated in horror, and the concept of a unilateral move towards student self-direction and control was quickly abandoned. What a foolish and damaging interpretation of an informative and valuable book!

Furthermore, what poor understanding of human nature. If teachers of older students plan to develop self-direction in students, *it must be because both the teacher and the students see the value in doing so.* They must also be willing to commit themselves to self-directed actions. If teachers of intermediate grade students (or older students) plan to share the responsibility for decision-making, they must see it as a gradual, developmental process. As with any developmental growth, the first step is small and progress may be slow.

For instance, setting aside ten or fifteen minutes of the school day as free-choice time is a technique for introducing decision-making skills to older students. The class would have the job of planning the use of that small period of time. As a first step, the teacher could guide decision-making by asking, "What are the things you could do during this period?" By answering this question students establish the options open to them (such as: study time, game time, talking time). At the end of that free time period, the teacher could lead a discussion about what did and did not go well during the free time. In discussing individual or group behavior, the students would focus on positive behavior models.

Another approach initiates free-choice time by telling the class that you want to involve them in planning for a fifteen minute free-choice time. You can explain that you are introducing this because you think that they should become more responsible for their own behavior. The class is then asked to identify what they could do during this time. What problems might (but not necessarily would) occur? What if some students wanted the room to be quiet and others wanted to listen to the record player, talk, and/or play games that created some noise? What if some students used the time to be rowdy?

At this point, you can present a fairly simple formula for problem solving: (1) identify the problem; (2) hypothesize three possible solutions to the problem; (3) select the first choice solution; (4) try that solution, and if it is not successful, try the next most popular solution until, if necessary, all three solutions are exhausted. Rarely will the first solution fail, but if it does there are two remaining. In the unusual event that all three hypotheses fail, then the class is faced with another problem solving situation: what will they do now? The four-step process will repeat itself. When the class has established effective management procedures for their free-choice time, the teacher can expand their opportunities for decision-making. Other areas for expansion would include: student planning for individual or small group projects; helping to plan part or all of the instructional day with the teacher; and finally (with some classes), developing processes for self-evaluation of student progress. Self-evaluation could even entail students participating in preparing their own report cards. William Glasser in his book, *Schools Without Failure* (Glasser, 1969) presents excellent ideas for student participation in self-evaluation of academic achievement.

Of course, role playing is useful with intermediate grade students. It is an excellent way to work through problems which arise. Furthermore, there are occasions when older students feel tht it is babyish to admit to anxieties and concerns. Acting provides a legitimate expression of those feelings without embarrassing the individual child. Older elementary grade students in particular hate to admit that they don't know how to behave in a specific situation; through class planning for acting-out the situation, participants, and purposes, these children can learn while saving face.

Another use for role playing is to broaden student understanding of children from other ethnic groups or their own ethnic group. By consciously setting about to determine the accurate, true characteristics of an ethnic group, myths are debunked and true knowledge and understanding begins.

You can identify the situation, participants, and purpose of the role playing. For example, you could identify the situation of a new student standing in the hallway of an all-white school. The new student is white and from an urban school in New York. His family has moved to this rural area because his father inherited a large home and several acres of land from an uncle. The new school is in a rural area where all of the families have lived for generations. At one time, coal mines had employed most of the town fathers, but the mines had shut down. Most of the students come from low socio-economic homes. There is only one church in the community, and all the families go to that church. Although a large city is only 100 miles away, very few students in the school have ever been there.

The participants in the situation are

the new student,

the principal, and

two students at the school.

The purpose of the communication is for the principal to introduce the new student, Leslie, to the two other students, John and Vince. The principal wants John and Vince to show Leslie around the school and make him feel welcome.

Your class should now identify stereotypes that are associated with whites. What are Anglos really like? How are John and Vince like Leslie? Would there be any differences in dress, in physical appearance, in dialect, in experiences? If so, what might those differences be? In my opinion, you should start with Anglos because people tend to lump all white people (as the use of the label, "Anglo," shows) in one mass group. Students can begin by realizing that differences in life experiences, differences in dialect, physical appearance, and expectations exist between *all* people regardless of their ethnic membership. This is as true for Anglos as it is for members of ethnic minority groups.

Similar situations can be set up with varying participants and ethnic groups. Of course, your class may have little actual knowledge about different cultures. They should identify what they may *think* they know and then discuss where and from whom they got their information. Is the information biased, does it stereotype, does it create prejudices?

The purpose of these role-playing sessions cannot be to develop *total* multicultural literacy. It can be to foster flexibility in thinking about other cultures, other world views, other value systems. And this fits in with organizing for instruction because children who seem insensitive to other people are children who cause trouble in the classroom.

Techniques for Developing Self-Control: Primary Grades

Primary grade children consistently surprise me with their ability to accept responsibility. The process of developing self-control and self-direction takes more time with some classes as well as with some children. And I must be honest and say that there are terrific highs and lows for the teacher. There will be days when a room of five-, six-, or seven-year-olds show incredible independence, and other days when you think, "Haven't they learned anything?" But this happens in even the most authoritarian classroom. The marvelous difference is that children who are involved in problem solving issues directly related to *their own behavior* are on their way to becoming *responsible human beings!* Think about it.

Organizing a room for Language Experience or for any other individualized program requires interest (learning) centers. So, one way of focusing on anticipating and channeling behavior is to introduce the care of interest centers as the childrens' responsibility.

As each game and activity is presented to the children, there should be a brief discussion of the appropriate care for these materials. Children can practice stacking and/or filing the materials, verbalizing what they are doing as they are doing it: "Big boxes go on the bottom. If you put little boxes on the bottom, the big boxes will be tippy and fall off." The children actually need to go through the role-playing process of organizing supplies, because simply *talking* about the methods of filing and stacking is too abstract for them to remember.

They will also learn, at a concrete level, that if they don't take care of their things, the consequence is that the games are removed from the room. The children must take care of the games, or the games will be put away until someone takes the responsibility for their care. After all, lack of care often leads to lost parts, torn game boards and crushed markers. That is not fair to children who will want to use the games next year.

Another technique teachers have used with developing responsible behavior in primary grade children is to establish the reason the students are in school. The teacher can begin by saying, "I am at this school and in this room because I want to help children learn. I know how to do this. I know where to get books. I know how to make games and other things that will help you learn to read and write and work with numbers. That is my job. Now, that is why I am here. Why are you here? What did you come here to do?" Some teachers have found that a stunned silence follows those questions. Very often children have not thought about why they are in school. They do not know what their *active* roles in education are. Now it becomes the teacher's responsibility to shift the child's preconceived notion of a passive role to an acknowledgment that the child is an active participant in learning and growing.

After the children have recovered from their initial surprise, the teacher asks again, "Why are you here?" The first response is, frequently, "To learn to read" or "To learn numbers." As the children begin to identify the reasons they are in school, the teacher can jot their exact words down on note paper. Later the teacher transcribes these notes onto large chart paper so that the responses can be seen easily. The statements that the children make are *their* commitment to their own education. The chart can be referred to when needed. It gives purpose and realism to the activities and lessons teachers prepare for and give to the children. "You said that you were here to learn to read, and now we are writing books. They will help you learn to read." All people function more effectively when they know why they are doing what they are doing. All people develop a stronger sense of self-reliance and responsibility when they believe and are shown that they are active participants in determining what is happening to them. If children have *no* responsibility for what determines their fate, then it follows that they have no responsibility for what is or isn't done.

An example of the continuing and practical use of this type of chart occurred in my first grade classroom just before Halloween. At the beginning of the year, we had discussed our purposes for being in school. I had written my purposes on chart paper and put them on the wall by my writing table. The children had dictated their purposes to me and I wrote them on chart paper. The children hung their charts by the front chalkboard. The first few weeks I would use both my chart and the children's charts as a method for group evaluation of daily progress. ("You said that you wanted to learn how to print. What did you do today that would help you learn to print?") The second month of school, the charts were not referred to. As that month progressed, I noticed that disruptive behavior was increasing. The children were interrupting me as I worked with individuals, games were being left out for me to put away, and the noise level was rising. I found myself becoming increasingly tired and cross. The children were relying more and more upon teacher direction and less and less on self-direction, but it was such a gradual process that no one seemed to be aware of what was happening. In the middle of one particular harrowing day, one of the first graders said, "I don't like it when you yell at us." I bit back a snappy reply, stopped the class, and requested a class meeting. I realized that things had come to a problem solving point. (I *was* yelling; I *wasn't* helping children to learn.)

"I have a problem, and I need your help. Jay said that I was yelling." I deliberately used facial expressions and body language which I hoped would tell them that I wasn't angry, but that I *was* concerned with the problem and did need help in solving it.

"Does my voice bother anyone else?"

Several children replied, very softly, "Yes."

"Okay, then I really do have a problem. I don't want to be loud and I don't want to sound like I am yelling at you. When is my voice too loud?"

"When you get mad—mostly after lunch."

This was a critical point since it would have been easy for me to say, "Yes, but if you were doing what you were supposed to be doing, I wouldn't have to get mad. If you don't want me to yell, don't you make me mad." I narrowly (because my pride was involved) avoided this serious error (serious because it probably would have caused severe damage to the trust between the children and me) by saying, "I think I need to look at my chart and see if I'm really doing what I'm supposed to be doing." The children listened while I read through my commitments listed on the chart. As I read, I commented about meeting my commitments. By and large, they were not really being met, and I said so. I asked, "What is happening? What am I doing?"

The children thought with me, and they all came to the conclusion that I was "bossing kids around."

"Is that my job? Am I here to boss kids around?"

"NO!"

"Who is supposed to boss you? Whose job is it to see that you do what you said you would do?"

"Ours."

"Well, let's look at your chart and see if you are bossing yourselves. Let's see if you are doing what you said you would do."

The class read over their chart. As they read, they came to the conclusion that they were not living up to their goals and commitments. The problem had been identified: each party not living up to commitments. Now, the next step was for the teacher and the students to decide what to do to solve the problem. As a group, we worked out possible solutions for the teacher (ignore children who weren't taking care of themselves, or ask the child, "What are you supposed to be doing?"). They solved the class problem by saying they needed to "Listen and take care of yourself."

With just a few exceptions, within the week we were happily involved in doing our jobs. Disruptive and overly dependent behavior lessened greatly and teacher "yelling" stopped. Everyone was busily working to meet their stated commitments. All of this took place because we planned to:

1. identify the purpose of teacher and child being in school,
2. establish who was responsible for what, and
3. develop mechanisms (such as class meetings) for solving problems that arise.

Primary grade children can expand their self-direction and control by helping to make class rules, arranging the desks and materials in the room, and planning their instructional day. Planning the day necessitates reviewing why they came to school in the first place. They will learn to plan a time for writing stories, doing math, reading, and studying science and social studies.

Every year my class would plan one or two days a month when they had a "messing-around day." On those days, they spent all of their time at learning centers, reading their books, singing with me, and simply relaxing with one another. Those were such good days. It gave us all time to absorb, to reflect on what we had been learning, to catch our breaths and get ready to move on.

Children are in school to learn, among other things, math, reading, and writing. Teachers are in school to provide the techniques children will need to develop in order to compute, read, and write. Teachers are there to provide most materials and resource information children will need in order to perfect basic skills and develop problem solving skills. Teachers must provide the necessary information, but it is children who must learn how to use that information. Students are responsible for *using* what they are taught and given. By focusing on student responsibilities and methods for meeting those responsibilities, most discipline problems are stopped before they begin. Children develop self-respect (because the teachers prove that they respect and trust them). They are becoming responsible decision makers and are learning how to meet commitments they make for themselves.

None of the suggestions made here are easy to follow. Declaring authoritarian control is much simpler—in the short run—because you don't have to go through the sometimes lengthy process of child decision-making. In all of the consideration of student commitment, the crux of the matter is teacher commitment. *To what, to whom are you committed?* Are you determined to help individuals grow with self-respect, responsibility, and the ability to think for themselves? If so, *no* approach is going to be easy, for you must trust yourself and your own judgment before you can trust and respect children to the degree that these procedures require. Trust yourself; trust your children.

Providing Materials for Independent Learning (Learning Centers)

Teachers need learning centers to meet individual needs of students, to provide opportunities for independent learning, and to help children learn self-direction. Teachers also need learning centers so that when students finish their Language Experience lessons, they have some place to go.

The ideas I will present are aids for making those materials. They include games and activity cards, and provide *planning* ideas for making the specific games and activity cards for your room.

Teaching and Practicing Skills

At all times all teachers should know what they are teaching. This is never more true than when they are teaching Language Experience and when they are using learning centers.

Each game or activity you make should provide *practice* with a skill or series of skills. Note the word "practice." I don't believe skills should necessarily be introduced through learning centers, but I do believe that students should practice skills during independent learning. Obviously, experimenting and hypothesizing should not be squelched, but practice is the goal.

Chapters for this book specify a sequence for skill development. These skills cover language arts and reading; consequently, they can be used as guidelines for making materials. There are other resources for identifying skills. These resources include:

Scope and Sequence Charts

District Student Learning Objectives (also known as Basic Competencies)

Using a Scope and Sequence Chart for Identifying Skills

Every major textbook series has developed a scope and sequence chart for each grade level textbook. It indicates the *parameters* of the information to be taught and the *sequence* in which the skills will be taught. In other words, the chart tells what will be taught and the order in which it will be taught. Scope and sequence charts are found both in the teacher's manual and (usually) on a large, single sheet provided by the publishing company. Some school districts adopt *one* reading series and use the scope and sequence chart (by grade level) as their student learning objectives.

The advantage of using the scope and sequence in a series is that you know that you are using material from a text written by authors considered to be authorities in the field. Furthermore, if the text is one adopted by your district, using the scope and sequence from the series insures your using teaching materials from a source sanctioned by your school district administration. I know of several teachers who use Language Experience as their reading/language arts program while using the adopted series as the resource for games and activities. They satisfy district requirements by using a specific reading series—their way. The tests found at the end of the chapters or sold with the series could be used in several ways: as tests/games to determine mastery; as activity cards for individual self-testing; and as tests to use after groups have worked through the games used for drill and practice.

Using Student Learning Objectives for Identifying Skills

Student learning objectives specify, in detail, the skills which are to be introduced and/or mastered at each grade level. An additional advantage of using student learning objectives is that teachers are assured that they will be teaching language arts and reading skills their district has specifically identified as being priority skills for teachers to teach and children to learn. These guides sometimes suggest using materials from several different textbook series adopted by the school district (called "multiple adoptions") or adopted by the state. Guides are excellent resources for developing ideas for games and activities. In using guides, as with all printed materials, the teacher must exercise judgment in evaluating whether or not all of the materials in a given resource are of use. Since texts, guides, and published materials in general are designed for a faceless, general audience, teachers must use their critical knowledge in the selection process. Each group of children has a special identity, unique needs, and abilities which published material cannot recognize. Standard materials presuppose a standard child. For instance, there are words, phrases, terms, and even sounds which are regional rather than national, and because of this teachers need to screen materials for their applicability to the children in the class.

Furthermore, many of these published materials (whether at the local or national level) do not always reflect the developmental nature of learning. Teachers must evaluate guides and texts to determine whether or not the tasks and concepts are representative of what they know their children both produce and understand.

Who Can Help Make Games and Activities?

One teacher cannot possibly make enough games and activities to cover an entire year's learning. Fortunately, it isn't necessary to begin the year with every game completed. The class will need games representative of the sequence of the specific language arts/reading skills; games which progress in degrees of difficulty. For example, if a class is studying the use of the dictionary, an initial activity might be to discover that words in the dictionary are arranged in a particular order. The next step might be to have the class discover that some words have more than one meaning, and a final step in the sequence might be for some students to learn the coding system used for identifying the linguistic origins of words. Resources such as scope and sequence charts and student learning objectives identify a sequence of skills which teachers can use in this first step of game-making. The class will need several games for each step in the sequence. Sometimes it will be best to make different versions of one game so that the individual children who need to work for an extended period of time on one sequential level can do so without becoming too familiar with one game. When teachers want to make duplicate games for work with groups of children, they can vary the appearance of the games by using different decorations and/or different titles. The games needed for the first month of school should be made before school starts. Games needed in January won't have to be made until November or December.

Teachers Can Help Each Other

A valuable resource for making games is one's fellow teacher. Teachers can discuss when, what, and how they should introduce, provide practice with, or test language arts/reading skills. Once this has been determined, the teachers could plan the format (the design for the game). Those using this approach will often include as many teachers as possible so that they can form an assembly line, each group of teachers responsible for making a certain number of copies of each game and then sharing the finished games with these teachers. This is a successful method because it is speedier and more efficient than if each teacher had tried to plan and make three entirely different games. It also means that teachers can borrow games from each other if they want to work with large groups of children.

Parents Can Help

There are many good reasons why parents should be asked to help prepare materials for student use. These reasons include:

1. It helps parents understand the teacher's educational goals and planning for their children.
2. It helps close the gap between school and home by directly involving parents and school. It forms a bond between the teacher, the children, and the parents.
3. It facilitates the teacher understanding of the community when they work informally with representatives of that community. It is a way of establishing contact.
4. It helps parents understand the enormous amount of preparation it takes to teach school, and that information goes back into the community.

However, there can be some difficulties in using parent volunteers. Potential problems to avoid include:

1. Parents may not be aware of the value teachers place upon the parents being at school on the day and at the time agreed upon. Concern with being precisely on time is not a cross-cultural value, so a compromise may have to be established.
2. Parents may not use good judgment in repeating what they hear or see at school. ("I noticed that _____ isn't doing the same work the other children are doing. . . .") A statement of that sort can hurt the child, the parent, and, ultimately, the teacher.
3. Parents may want to visit to talk about their child while the teacher is trying to teach everyone's children.
4. Parents may decide that they should be teaching rather than helping.
5. Teachers may not provide clear directions for the parents to follow.
6. Teachers may not be sensitive to a parent's apprehension about making mistakes in front of a teacher.
7. Parents may become embarrassed because other teachers in the building are not aware that they are volunteer workers.

Suggestions teachers might want to follow in order to avoid these problems include:

1. Teachers should have a conversation with parent volunteers which will help them to understand your needs and expectations. (It will also help you understand the parent's needs and expectations.)
2. Teachers should discuss with volunteers the importance they place upon protecting children from being hurt by casual comments or remarks taken back into the community.
3. Teachers should prepare a work area for the volunteer. This area should have all of the materials the volunteer will need.

4. Teachers should have models, illustrations and/or clearly stated directions for the games. Models for either the correct form for printing or the correct form for cursive must be included.
5. Teachers should introduce the volunteer parent to the personnel in the school.

These suggestions are not designed to discourage teachers from asking parents into their room. They are included to make teachers aware of their responsibility in preventing misunderstandings.

Retired People Can Help

Children can benefit greatly by being with people who are of retirement age. Growing older should be a positive experience. If retired people are willing to come into the schools, teachers are not only tapping a marvelous resource but they are telling their students that they value older people.

Ask for volunteers from older people who live in the school community. If there are bilingual/bicultural children in the class, ask for a volunteer who speaks the same combination of languages. A bilingual/bicultural volunteer is a valuable resource person for everyone in the class.

Students Can Help

There are students in every classroom who can make games. In fact, some teachers plan to have the students in their classes make all of their own games. Teachers can also ask teachers from other grades if they have students who would be efficient volunteers. This is another opportunity to benefit from bilingual/bicultural resource people. Often both the other teachers and the students will be eager to help; however, teachers will need to use some caution since some colleagues will volunteer a student simply because that student is a discipline problem for that teacher.

Teachers must be as organized and thorough with the student volunteers as with the parent volunteers. The same preplanning to avoid misunderstandings will be necessary.

Materials: Where to Get Them

Materials for making games need not be expensive. There is some cost involved, but teachers should look for means to defray expenses.

Sometimes parent organizations, such as the Parent Student Teacher Association (PSTA), have small amounts of money available for teachers to use. Teachers should also ask their principal if there is any money which the school can contribute (such as money from the school carnival or small sums allotted for expendable, instructional supplies).

Workbooks/Textbooks

Districts invariably have copies of old workbooks and textbooks which are earmarked for disposal. Explore the school for potential discards. School warehouses and textbook depositories often have textbooks and workbooks teachers can either take or buy for a nominal fee. Books can be torn or cut into single sheets, glued to a solid backing, covered with clear contact and used for individual activities. The tests in workbooks and texts can be torn out and used for evaluating and diagnosing individual progress through a series of unit lessons.

Teachers may want to collate activities from different books for sequential, easy-to-difficult activities.

Textbook companies often have free samples of new texts and workbooks which they are willing to send to teachers. If there is a charge, it is low enough so that the book is still a reasonable purchase.

Wrapping Paper and Greeting Cards

Alphabet games, nursery rhyme games, themes for games, and decorations for games can be made from gift wrapping paper and greeting cards. Wrapping paper and greeting cards are, at this time, one of the best resources for pictures of children from different ethnic groups. Educational materials such as workbooks and textbooks do not have many quality illustrations of children who are representative of different ethnic groups. When quality illustrations do appear in books, it is painful even to think of tearing them up for a game. Whether or not a class is ethnically diverse, all educational materials, including games, should reflect diversity.

Sex stereotyping still occurs in many textbook and workbook illustrations, and the aware teacher will need to look to many sources, such as wrapping paper and greeting cards, for less stereotyped pictures.

Sticker Fun Books

Sticker fun books are particularly handy for those of us who lack artistic ability. These books are not only attractive, they are easy to use. Usually one sticker fun book will make two or more games, and the cost is less than one dollar for each book.

The Whitman sticker fun books have begun to include ethnically diverse pictures in their publications. Other sources for multi-ethnic materials are Golden Book sticker stamp books.

All of these books can be used simply to decorate games or to give a theme to games. Entire games can also be built around one book. For example, books on birds, dinosaurs, and sea life could be used for creative writing, as illustrations for research topics, for classification, for matching or card games. Sticker fun folk tale books could be used to stimulate story writing, creative dramatics, or for testing listening and sequencing skills. The books could be used to correlate games with entire units of lessons—for instance, folk tale games with folk tale lessons.

Recipe Cards

Recipe cards or file cards come in different sizes and colors. They are particularly useful for card games and matching games. They can be stored in small file boxes or recipe boxes. Many teachers can order both the cards and the file boxes from the school district supply offices.

Manila Folders and Library Card Pockets

Schools have supplies of manila folders and library card pockets. Ease of accessibility is not the only advantage of these materials; they also lend themselves to self-contained, easily stored, individualized games. For instance, if the class is working on building a sight word vocabulary, these words can be written in squares on the inside of the folder, with matching word cards stored in a library card pocket on the back of the folder. Different versions of this game could be developed for bilingual/bicultural children; they would match a word from one language with the same word in a second (or first language).

For specific activities, a card or a sequence of cards can be stored on the left side of the inside of the folder. When the students complete work, they can insert their answers under a paper clip on the right side of the folder. The back of the folder can have a lined check sheet where the students can write their name and the date the activity was started and completed. The teacher would record the data when the completed work was evaluated. An organizational procedure such as this frees a student from waiting for the teacher to review work during class time. It is also a fast way for teachers to go through and evaluate student performance of a specific learning skill.

Entire units of work can be created and stored using this procedure. The folders can be color-coded or numbered so that they would represent a developmental progression through a series of lessons.

Markers for Games

Markers are used in games to move from "start" to "finish." Therefore, in planning games which involve both a game board and movement along the game board, teachers need to provide markers for the students to use. Almost anything can be used as a marker; here are a few examples of objects some teachers have devised:

- small student-decorated rocks
- bottle caps
- odds and ends from discarded games
- tokens
- nut shells
- small wooden cubes or beads
- tiny airplanes, cars or similar toys

Posterboard for Game Boards

Posterboard makes an excellent game board. It comes in many attractive colors, is relatively sturdy, and most schools keep it in stock. Posterboard can be purchased at stores which carry art supplies, office supplies, or school supplies. It usually costs less than fifty cents a sheet. One sheet can make one large game or it can be cut into four smaller game boards. Games made from posterboard should last several years.

Preserving the Games

Making games is both time consuming and laborious. It is foolhardy to invest energy and time in any project of this sort unless time is also invested in planning for the maintenance and preservation of games.

Whenever games are used by children, there will be grubby fingers, accidental spills, misplaced footsteps, and all of the other hazards associated with use. It is up to the teacher to make the games durable. Children should enjoy the use of these things without constantly having to be warned and admonished by the teacher. This is not to say that the students have no responsibility in caring for the materials in their classroom; it is to say that teachers need to make durable materials, knowing how they will be used.

Lamination

Lamination is an effective process for adding years to the life of games made from paper products. When it is used it creates a shiny, durable finish which often enhances colors. Since laminating involves the use of heat, teachers must be careful that there are no air pockets between the materials being used and the laminating film. Air pockets create steam, and the steam may cause colors to spot or run.

Clear Contact Paper

Clear contact paper can be purchased by the roll. It usually comes either with a shiny or with a dull finish. For most games a dull finish is fine, but for colorful materials, shiny contact paper is by far the better product.

Whether teachers use contact paper or lamination, both sides of the game should be covered. The back will receive almost as much scuffing and use as the top. In placing contact paper on the materials to be covered, carefully pre-measure and plan the procedure. Once in place, contact paper sticks—firmly!

Car Upholstery Fabric

Teachers have made huge bingo games, word games, math games, and alphabet games on pieces of either plastic or vinyl car upholstery. The advantage of this type of material is that it is easy to store and it is durable. A disadvantage is that some types of ink will bead rather than mark the surface. Teachers who have used car upholstery have gotten inexpensive scraps from businesses which specialize in upholstering cars.

Storage

Games and activities made on manila folders, or cut from workbooks are easy to store. They can be placed upright in cardboard boxes where they are readily visible. The cardboard boxes can be decorated so that they are not only attractive but also so that the children can tell at a glance the contents of the box.

Recipe boxes or file boxes make it simple to store materials written on file cards. There should be an established method for marking these boxes. Students must be able to find materials they will use frequently and *independently*.

Posterboard can be stored by putting up hooks in the room. After using a paper punch to make holes in the corners of the board, teachers can hang games on the hooks where they will be visible but out of the way.

Wherever or however the games are stored, they should be kept out of heavily trafficked areas. Games that are no longer in use should be removed from the room and stored in cabinets.

Resources for Ideas

Complete Guide to Learning Centers. Susan B. Petreshene, Pendragon House, 2898 Joseph Ave., Campbell, Ca. 95008. (The best, most practical, comprehensive resource on the market)

The Great Perpetual Learning Machine. Jim Blake and Barbara Ernst. Little Brown and Company, 1976.

Workjobs. Mary Baratta-Lorton. Addison-Wesley, 1972. (Teachers of primary grade children love this book.)

Language Arts Activities. Iris and Sidney Tiedt. Allyn and Bacon, 1978.

The Great Learning Book, Ages 8–18. Ann Rahnasto Bogojavlensky and Donna Grossman. Addison-Wesley, 1977. (Superior.)

Reading Activities for Middle and Secondary School. Carl Smith and Peggy Elliot. Holt, Rinehart and Winston, 1979.

Reading for Survival in Today's Society, Volumes 1 and 2. Anne Flowers, Ann H. Adams and Elsa E. Woods. Goodyear, 1978. (A must for upper elementary and secondary.)

Room Arrangements for Maximum Space and Minimum Confusion

With projections of increased numbers of students per teacher, wise use of space becomes more important. Teachers and students must use space optimally.

First you need to decide on the number of learning centers you plan to set up. My advice (if this is new to you) is, start slowly. First-year teachers or teachers who have never done this before should plan on having a reading and writing center. It will take enough time and energy to stock and implement just these two centers in one year. If you begin with reading and writing centers, put them in a quiet spot away from the pencil sharpener, wastebasket, and door to the room.

As you progress, you can add:

A listening center (you may have tapes, earphones, a record player, etc.).

An art center (with oil and water base clay, paints, paper, glue, junk boxes of material scraps, yarn, needles, and sturdy materials for stitchery pictures, etc.).

A science center (featuring a variety of materials for experimenting).

A math center (providing manipulative as well as pencil and paper activities).

A music center (with musical instruments, such as an autoharp, tone bells, tambourines, drums, record player).

A social studies center (with study prints, magazines, globes, maps, artifacts).

You can also put up temporary centers that reflect a current topic of interest to the students.

Interest centers can be made by pushing two desks together; by bringing smaller tables into the area; by turning boxes over and covering them with butcher paper; and by building boxes from scrap wood. Storage for games and activities within the centers could be in cardboard boxes, plastic tubs, and (as I saw in an ESL class) attractive baskets of different sizes.

I usually put centers in the corners of the room with noisy centers by noisy areas. I think the most important factor to consider is noise reduction. However you plan the room arrangement, make sure that quiet areas are not next to noisy, heavily-trafficked areas.

Sometimes you will need to break away from a more traditional concept of room arrangement in order to use your space well. If you put desks in clusters, you can open up more floor space. Flexible room arrangements allow easy access to desks, materials, and centers for children who are on crutches or in wheelchairs. Students who are visually or hearing impaired can sit where they are closest to the sounds and sights of instruction. Those easily distracted students can be seated in quiet, less busy areas. Screens can be made to provide quiet, private areas.

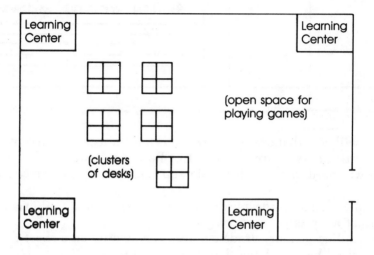

To develop problem solving skills and teach children to channel their own behavior, they should as much as possible be directly involved in planning the positioning of desks and centers.

You may want to screen off a center or a part of the room for added quiet. You can create a screen by cutting open one side of a refrigerator box (or any other large appliance box, obtained from a local appliance store). Students can decorate the screen with paintings and drawings. Now, are you saying that you can't trust students to behave behind the screen? Reread the first part of this chapter.

Using Centers

If you are worried about students all going to the same center, don't. By using the simple device of sign-up sheets, you can control congestion. Have students write their names on an interest-center sheet as soon as they arrive in the morning. Older students can simply sign under the appropriate category.

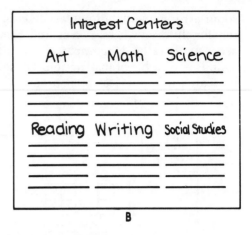

Interest Centers	
Reading	Math

A

Interest Centers		
Art	Math	Science
——————	——————	——————
Reading	Writing	Social Studies
——————	——————	——————

B

You will note that example B restricts the number at each center to five participants; there are only five lines per center. You and the class will need to decide if the sign-up is for one day, two days, and so on.

Keep the sign-up sheets so that you can be certain that everyone works at a variety of centers.

Prereading primary grade children can sign up on a sheet that is categorized by a drawing that represents that area.

Art	Science
Toshiko	Matt
Tony	Kristine
Mike	Wendy
Beth	Chris
Dao	Andreas
$1+1=2$ Math	Reading
Maria	Jaun
Anna	Johanna
Susumu	Noburu
Sophia	Lily
Paulo	Eric

Smooth use of the centers must be preceded by having the class discuss the purpose of the center and *their* responsibility in using and maintaining all of the centers.

Keeping a Record of the Use of Games

One method of keeping track of the use of games has been described: attaching a check sheet to the back of individual games made on folders. Using the skills suggested for the chapters in this book is yet another method for keeping a record of student use of games. Games can be categorized according to the general skills they teach (listening, speaking, reading, and writing). A recording sheet can be sequenced to match the skill sequence within those general categories. The teacher can evaluate and check off each student's use of the individual games as that game was completed. Since the checklist is headed "Activity and Date," the teacher would simply indicate the game, code the pupil's performance and enter the date of completion.

Listening Skill	Activity and Date			
Identifying use of pitch	Tape # 4 ⓒ 10/15/82	Tape #5 Ⓡ 3/17/82		
stress, pause, intonation				

Aside from keeping a record of pupil progress, this procedure also prevents a teacher from repeatedly assigning the student the same game.

Concluding Thoughts

Organizing a room requires thought and time. It necessitates a teacher believing that students can be responsible, and that they can be trusted. Obviously, it takes time; but in the *end* it is worth every second of planning!

Pertinent Resources

Bader, L. A. *Reading Diagnosis and Remediation in Classroom and Clinic.* New York: Macmillan, 1980.

Baratta-Lorton, M. *Workjobs.* Menlo Park, CA: Addison-Wesley, 1972.

Blake, J., and Ernst, B. *The Great Perpetual Learning Machine.* Boston: Little, Brown and Co., 1976.

Bogojavlensky, A. R., and Grossman, D. R. *The Great Learning Book.* Menlo Park, CA: Addison-Wesley, 1977.

Freedman, M., and Perl, T. *A Sourcebook for Substitutes and Other Teachers.* Menlo Park, CA: Addison-Wesley, 1974.

Glasser, W. *Schools Without Failure.* New York: Harper and Row, 1969.

———. *Reality Therapy.* New York: Harper and Row, 1965.

Petreshene, S. S. *Complete Guide to Learning Centers.* Palo Alto: Pendragon House, 1978.

Shaftel F. and Shaftel, G. *Role-Playing for Social Values.* Englewood Cliffs: Prentice-Hall, 1967.

Smith, C. B., and Elliott, P. G. *Reading Activities for Middle and Secondary Schools: A Handbook for Teachers.* New York: Holt, Rinehart and Winston, 1979.

Tiedt, S. W. and Tiedt, I. M. *Language Arts Activities for the Classroom.* Boston: Allyn and Bacon, Inc., 1978.

Finally. . . .

The end of the circle has become the starting point. Beginning learners have grown into intermediate learners while the latter move on to progressively sophisticated levels of expression. Lessons that they have learned through writing spin back to speaking; speech becomes more refined through the conscious application of learning gained through writing. So, the cycle starts again.

Language Experience generates excitement, enthusiasm, and eagerness in students and teachers alike. Every day opens new doors to learning and independence. It is difficult for me to describe the difference that Language Experience has made in me as a teacher. I can remember becoming bored with the endless repetition of basal texts, and finding it difficult to sustain student reading interest.

When I began teaching Language Experience, this changed. Learning became an unfolding of self-respect, thinking, and creative expression. The children expanded my knowledge and understanding of their world view. Individual differences became a source of pride and accomplishment. I have never ceased to bless the day that my son and I met Evawynne Spriggs, who took our hands and led us into her beautiful world of teaching. Eric continues to write and believe in himself as a writer and a composer. He has never lost that spark that was found and cherished fourteen years ago. He has sustained his ability to think and problem-solve—and so, I hope, have I.

This book was written in hopes that the excitement and joy that my students, son, other teachers, and I shared through Language Experience could, in turn, be shared with others.

People use Language Experience in different ways. Some begin their teaching using Language Experience as their total language arts and reading program. Others integrate it with a basal program. Which way is best? Well, if we truly believe in individual differences there can be only one answer. You must decide, because the best way for you is the best way to use Language Experience.

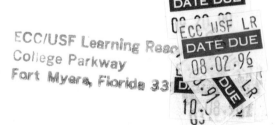